EDUCATION for SURVIVAL
More than just a memory game

ROGER WAIGH

THE CHOIR PRESS

Copyright © 2022 Roger Waigh

All rights reserved. No part of this publication may be reproduced or transmitted in any form or by any means, electronic or mechanical including photocopying, recording or any information storage or retrieval system, without prior permission in writing from the publishers.

The right of Roger Waigh to be identified as the author of this work has been asserted by him in accordance with the Copyright, Designs and Patents Act 1988

First published in the United Kingdom in 2022
by The Choir Press

ISBN 978-1-78963-281-1

**For Sally, Cathy and Paul, Tom
and Emily, Bron and Ollie**

with special thanks to Brian and Ursula Murdoch for providing a different perspective and suggestions on improving the text.

There is nothing new in this book, merely a series of reminders of aspects of education that have been forgotten, or set aside by 'experts'.

The following quotation is from 'On Learning Golf' by Percy Boomer, first published in 1946 and still being reprinted: his father was a village schoolmaster in Jersey.

As an educationist he was generations ahead of his time. He saw no use in forcing a boy to try to learn subjects which he was obviously incapable of absorbing - and of which he could make no use anyway, but he did help his pupils to develop such talents and natural aptitudes as they possessed.

This encapsulates the main theme of this book, with a reminder that it is not just the subject that matters but the way that it is delivered.

Contents

Foreword	1
Basic concepts	5
For the teachers	9

The broad principles

Memory versus logic	12
The learning slope	16
Frameworks	17
Learning by rote	19
The age of knowledge	20
Breadth versus depth	22
Learning to swim	31
Aptitudes	33
Wise versus clever	38
Curiosity	40
Understanding	42
Communication skills	45
Dialects	48
Responsibility	51
Discipline	54
Practical skills	56

Learning in school

| A philosophical conundrum | 58 |

Parents	61
Punishment	63
Learning later in life	67
Exercise and the school week	70
Food	74

Learning in universities

University funding	77
Being an academic	81
The class system	83
The research assessment exercise	87
Uniformity of thought	94
Big Pharma	96
Techniques	103
Grit	105
Exam format	109
Computer Assisted Learning	113

Subject by subject

Religion	114
Science	121
Scientists	128
Practical classes	131
Ecology	135
Modern Languages	138
Music	140

Art	144
Management	145
Economics	150
Personal finances	156
Advertising	159
Politics	162
Anthropology: the hunter-gatherer	166
The greenhouse effect	169

Generalities

Exam technique	172
The year in education	173
The cult of celebrity	174
Overseas aid	177
Having children	184
Leisure	186

External factors

Immigration	189
Drugs	191
Health and Safety	194

Epilogue 196

Foreword

I started teaching in the first year of my PhD, in 1966. I was asked to teach in a physical chemistry lab, a subject that was very badly taught when I was an undergraduate; so badly that I had scarcely understood any of it. I needed the money so I agreed to do it, but first I had to come to terms with the material being taught, which had not changed since I took the same course three years before.

To my surprise, on closer inspection it was not as difficult as I had imagined and I felt confident in explaining the basic concepts behind conductimetric titration, for example. The difference was that I could give my whole attention to it, with a compelling reason to do so.

In 1970 I started my first permanent university appointment, as a lecturer in Pharmaceutical Chemistry, and over the next few years formed the heretical opinion that the chemistry required by pharmacy students was not the same as that taught in departments of chemistry. I could not see why our students needed to know about the Grignard reaction, for example.

After a couple of years I was entrusted with a third year course on heterocyclic chemistry, lasting for six lectures, which was historically pure chemistry, of little relevance to a health-based profession, so I asked for permission to change the course in a radical manner. I think the students were a little surprised, but they could not argue about the relevance.

Instead of lectures, I asked one of the students to open the British Pharmacopeia at random and write the nearest chemical structure on the blackboard. I then asked the class to copy the structure and make some simple predictions about pharmaceutically relevant properties such as solubility and stability in water, whether the compound would absorb UV light at a useful wavelength for analysis, and so on.

The results showed that as a group they did not have a clue. Some of their predictions showed, for example, a complete lack of understanding of the concepts of acidity and basicity as relevant to organic molecules. This is of fundamental importance in understanding the way that medicines behave when swallowed: the stomach contents are strongly acidic but elsewhere the pH is close to neutral, which affects how drugs are absorbed and pass around the body.

I gave them six randomly selected compounds to think about in the hour or so allocated, collected in the sheets with their responses and took them home to look through. In the next slot I handed back their work and went through the examples, so they could annotate what they had done, and told them that the next session would follow the same pattern. In all there were six sessions of a little under an hour each.

They were good students and learned quickly. By the third session their answers were making more sense. It was clear that they felt more confident, an essential part of any learning process. Compared to the old course, which had simply been one of my colleagues talking to them so that they could make notes, the students were actively involved.

The other advantages were

(a) The material was relevant to their future career

(b) There was adequate repetition

(c) Feedback was given soon after the challenge

(d) It had some novelty value compared to the usual lecture course

(e) The random element in selecting the examples emphasised that the concepts were of wide applicability

(f) Setting exam questions was easy and did not require just factual recall.

From my point of view, the biggest reward was that they began to understand the chemistry and how it might relate to their future work. Given any previously unseen drug structure they could make useful predictions, an important step forward from the previous expectation that they would merely respond like blotting paper to the mass of information supplied to them. The key was understanding, critically supported by repetition, so that the approach could be seen to be consistent, which built confidence.

A short time later, I tried setting a problem on a final year exam paper which was designed to test understanding rather than recall. It was a disaster. The students had not been prepared for it and could not do it, which taught me a lesson: if the exam is about depth of understanding the breadth has to be reduced. They need time for swimming lessons, not just to be thrown in the deep end.

An objection raised by some of my colleagues was that the students needed to know x and y and z. My answer was that if they cover the whole alphabet to pass the exam they will not distinguish the critical information, the things they need to understand and retain, from the inessential detail. With no priorities they quickly forget the whole lot. Very quickly, as in Friday to Monday.

Having started to write this book, the subject matter broadened far beyond my initial ambition. From an initial intention to explore the means for a student to survive in the modern world and for the UK to survive by making best use of the capabilities of her citizens, it became apparent that survival would ultimately depend on an appreciation of what it means to be human. You may disagree with some of my conclusions but I hope not all of them.

There is some repetition of the basic concepts from chapter to chapter, in different contexts; it is intended that each chapter can be read in isolation.

Roger Waigh

September 2022

Basic concepts

In the 20th century, the means of providing life skills tended to concentrate on information, supplied and assessed through the written word, rather than practical experience. This runs counter to the whole history of humankind, which from earliest times provided education by practical example. Skills have tended to be replaced by facts, transiently remembered and often unrelated to the necessity to earn a living.

Any system of education should be questioned if it encourages young people, with no inherited wealth, to devote several of their formative years to subjects of no material value. I am not saying that the less privileged should never make such a commitment but they should be aware of the implications. To treat them like the sons of landowners, who in earlier times could be sent on a European tour, having studied ancient languages to the exclusion of everything else, is not appropriate. The absence of any practical knowledge does not matter to those who are born wealthy, since they may be supported by their family.

From the individual's point of view, studying subjects that do not help in getting a job, to the exclusion of all others, is probably unwise. This is not a Philistine viewpoint: if you can earn a living as an accountant while spending your free time reading the early Greek philosophers you are free to do so, but it is common for those who choose a purely academic subject at university to avoid that subject later in life, as they make progress in the activities that allow them to eat.

Generally speaking, the parts of a specialist subject that relate to everyday life are hidden in the mass of information that forms the 'syllabus'. A perception that many areas of study require vast factual detail leads, paradoxically, to specialisation at an early stage. As a result and purely for exemplification, many people in modern Britain know nothing of microbiology, despite the impact that microbes have on their lives. It should not be necessary to have a degree, or any kind of exam qualification in biology, to be familiar with the difference between a virus and a bacterium. This matters when you have a cold. The same could be said about a variety of subjects that are ignored in the general syllabus. Very recently, widespread ignorance of the way the human body defends itself against infection has led some to question the value of immunisation using vaccines. Conspiracy theories abound, fertilised by misunderstanding and baseless fear.

For the optimal functioning of society, having citizens who do not demand antibiotics to treat a cold will be beneficial. Even more useful, having citizens who are numerate and can manage their own finances will prevent much distress. For example, the concepts of 'percentage' and 'Annual Percentage Rate ' should be familiar to everybody, allowing informed decisions about borrowing money, for example. To reach this goal requires more than just a lesson and an exam.

The accepted way to educate our population is based on the needs of commerce in Victorian society, essentially reading, writing and arithmetic. To some extent these needs have been forgotten, to the point where numbers of children leave school without being able to read or write and with no sense of number. The desire to make society more egalitarian, in principle admirable, has led to an unchallenged assumption that the processes that suit a small number of academics can be applied to the majority. In some subjects this can lead to a merit order based on the individual's ability to absorb masses of facts and describe them to an examiner. If you are very good at this you may shine as a student but find the transition to the 'real' world rather difficult.

Part of the problem lies in the exam system, which requires a frantic attempt to get as many half-understood facts as possible on paper in a short time; never, in the life that follows, will this be a useful skill. The exam system has led to a teaching programme that requires topics to be 'covered', even though retention is minimal. If students quickly forget everything they have learned, what is the point?

With different teaching methods and different assessment protocols, the 'order of merit' could change very substantially. Those who were top may come bottom, while those who were regarded as stupid may shine. The question is: 'Which order of merit best reflects the modern needs of society?'. If we fail to adapt, the principles of natural selection will favour other cultures, in other parts of the world.

Education in other parts of the world may seem irrelevant but it affects the prospects for the UK as a whole and not simply in the competition for technical advancement. There is constant pressure from the developing world for people to move to the UK, despite overcrowding and resistance from the indigenous people. Rapid population growth in Africa and elsewhere will eventually constitute a major tragedy for mankind, beyond the potential failure to provide food. Population pressure leads to loss of forests, a major factor in climate change, and general degradation of productive land. Invariably, when women are educated and encouraged to think, they tend to have smaller families.

For the teachers

At times in the past, when I have dared to question the effectiveness of our national teaching methods, I have been assailed by a variety of members of the teaching profession, who take criticism very personally. My suggestions are not directed at the people who deliver at what used to be the chalk face: I can say, from deeply held belief and personal experience, that teachers are among the most important people in society. A good teacher can inspire students to follow a path that leads to a better life.

For good teachers to thrive, the learning environment needs to be organised. First, it is necessary that teachers be paid well, so that there is competition for vacancies. If teaching ceases to be attractive, there is a danger that positions cannot be filled or those who are appointed are lacking in motivation and/or expertise.

The second essential for effective teaching is that disruption must be kept to a minimum. Some disruption may be avoided if the environment is not overly academic: it is best that the kids can see some point in what they are doing. However, there are children who have not been controlled at home and who think that the same anarchy can be brought to the classroom. These disrupters have to be removed if the others are to be given a fair chance.

Continuing this theme, trying to teach mixed ability classes is a dead loss for everybody. The quick learners are held back and the slow coaches are made to feel inferior, which leads to resentment and sometimes bullying. In this context, **it is important to remember that the quick ones may simply be thriving because the approach suits them**. Those who like to come to terms with French irregular verbs may struggle if asked to wire a simple electronic circuit. If the only teachers available are capable of teaching French but not electronics there is a strong probability that the school will not produce any electronic engineers.

A failure to pay teachers properly and to give them productive working conditions ensures that children from poorer backgrounds are educationally neglected. Families with more disposable income can afford, sometimes with difficulty, to pay for their children to attend a school where the teachers have a relatively easy time. Poorer parents have to accept whatever is on offer, even if the school has a high proportion of increasingly violent children, who have no intention of learning anything.

Some will argue that the ability to pay for their children's schooling is a reward for the parent's hard work and sacrifices, but the consequence is to throw talent away by giving some children very little chance of a better life. Surely we need to get the best out of everybody?

This logic also applies to the '11 plus' system. It must be wrong to select at an early age and discard the rest, especially when those who fail are very likely to do so because the academic system does not suit them.

It is possible to imagine a school that does not confine the children to long hours in the classroom, without abandoning the intention to pursue serious education. I used to enjoy woodwork and found what I had learned useful, although it had little status in a heavily academic school. The status of different activities is a problem in the UK, an indicator of a class system that has refused to wither, despite the recognition that a plumber can earn far more than a librarian. The old aristocratic dismissal of those who earn a wage has been passed down to many in the population, who think that a lawyer is 'superior' to a bricklayer or an engineer.

These themes are developed in the pages that follow but first there is one important general point to be made. After food, shelter and being part of a group, the next human desire is for respect; this is even more important than sex. Irrespective of the work they do, people thrive on respect. At one time, those who had a university education tended to be given respect automatically. That tendency is fading fast, as we approach 50% of school leavers being funnelled into academic tertiary education, with many unable to find any enhanced employment opportunities.

For education to succeed, both teacher and pupil need to respect each other. and to respect the needs of the country.

The broad principles

Memory versus logic

When I was growing up there was a man called Leslie Welch who could remember all the details of sporting events. He earned a living as an entertainer, the 'Memory Man'. It is said that he was the star of eight Royal Command performances, 4,000 radio appearances, 500 television shows and 12 films for Twentieth Century Fox (John Barber, through the internet).

Today, it is possible to answer questions on University Challenge on a variety of subjects including ancient Greek myths, US presidents or the colours of flags. If you can answer these questions very quickly you may be called a genius. The same applies to 'Master Mind', 'Brain of Britain' and every other quiz show.

While it is possible that somebody with an excellent memory and rapid recall may be a genius, such a conclusion is not remotely justified without more evidence. A genius must be able to think constructively and use imagination to reach useful conclusions. If these abilities happen to go with an outstanding memory it is a coincidence.

And yet in some important subjects we base our system of education on the learning of facts, pure and simple. I had assumed this to be largely true in the 'sciences' and was surprised when James Loewen described a similar phenomenon in the teaching of history in the USA (see under 'Breadth versus depth').

On this theme, in my own subject, I have two contrasting examples from real life:

William (not his real name) came to one of Britain's best universities to study a scientific subject. William did not take kindly to the requirement to learn screeds of facts, which formed the basis of the first year's study. He failed his first year exams, failed the September resit, and was sent away for a year. He came back to resit the first year exams and passed, so entered the second year.

At the end of the second year he did the same thing, failed his exams and the resit, so he left for another year. Once more he passed the resit and was allowed to enter the final year. Unfortunately, under the university's rules he was no longer eligible for an honours degree, but sat the same exams as all the honours students. At this stage of his chequered career he selected an option with a great emphasis on problem solving. The external examiner, having seen the papers for the whole group, described William as 'clearly the outstanding student'.

Claire (again not her real name) followed a similar course to William, in a different university. Confronted with similar problem-solving classes, she said 'I can't do this, but give me stuff to learn and I will get a first'. Which she did.

Which of these graduates is likely to be the most useful in the community? We cannot say, but something has gone wrong when memory is prized above all.

One reason for the system that we have arrived at in many areas of education is that it is easier and cheaper to measure memory rather than other abilities. In essence, the only way that a clear thinker can make career progress in some subject areas is to be blessed with an excellent memory, even in an age when so much information is available at the touch of a button.

Have a look at an exam paper, in any subject that is front-loaded with facts, at any level, and you will find an emphasis on recall. A partial exception is maths, which lends itself to problem solving, but even here practice, allied to a good memory, makes a big difference in passing exams. There is simply not time, in a maths exam, to work out the answers from first principles. It is more effective to recognise the nature of the problem and apply an acquired method, from memory.

It is common for top exam results to be a poor indicator of ability in the workplace, simply because the answers to workplace problems can rarely be learned beforehand. It is not uncommon for a research leader or an industrial employer to say that he or she prefers not to take first-class honours graduates. Of course, this is unfair on those who happen to be imaginative thinkers as well as having good memories. On the other hand, one UK researcher that I knew well said that his best PhD student had a third class honours degree from Hong Kong.

Of course knowledge is essential, but a student who gets poor grades as an undergraduate may be able to absorb the important stuff, while not retaining the unimportant detail that leads to high marks. If he or she is lucky, progress may follow in a different environment but this is more difficult than it should be. As a generalisation, I think that those who devise a syllabus should spend a lot more time discussing the true significance of much that is to be taught, with a view to keeping the fact load to manageable proportions and allocating more time to fundamentals. With time for repetition between terms and between years.

The learning slope

Everybody can learn but typically people are classified according to the speed at which they learn. Those who are slow need a shallow slope and tend to be regarded as stupid, while the ones who ascend a steep slope quickly are thought to be intelligent. This is damaging and wrong.

Some people are cautious thinkers, wanting to check and cross-check their thought processes to avoid mistakes. They will choose a shallow slope, if possible. Those who think more deeply may also choose a shallow slope because they do not trust any process that involves jumping to conclusions; they may investigate aspects of a problem that would not occur to others. Thinking deeply is challenging and a wise person will take as much time as is needed. Of course, exams tend to reward the risk-takers, who think quickly and make mistakes but who complete the paper.

A teacher can try to persuade a cautious thinker to answer questions more quickly but this is not easy; caution is a personality trait. In the real world it is usually possible to give more time to a problem than is allocated in an exam and the quick mind may make mistakes that prove costly. There is room for a range of mind types in approaching a task, as long as they talk to each other; one person's flash idea can be analysed and dissected more slowly, to reach a sound and productive conclusion. It is the exam that needs to be examined.

Frameworks

Trying to learn anything in isolation is very difficult. If your previous experience does not allow you a shallow slope in coming to terms with something new there is a tendency to give up. Even very bright minds can erect barricades to whole areas of human understanding if the learning process is too steep. For some, this can mean a rejection of anything 'sciency' or a near total failure to handle numbers.

It is the teacher's task to make barriers surmountable but it is important to distinguish between learning for academic success and learning for everyday use. Every person needs to have a framework of understanding in all the significant areas of knowledge, before they can make sense of it.

In many cases, it is only the framework that remains when all else is forgotten. This is perfectly natural but the residue of familiarity, and the feeling that something is not frightening, are important. When we have the background, rusty though it may be, we can absorb new information as it becomes significant.

If the approach to a new topic is surrounded in mystery it may be rejected, with the student feeling depressed at being so stupid. Nothing is too difficult, if it is approached in a gradual manner, for most people to get a reasonably accurate idea of what it is all about. Perhaps quantum mechanics should be excluded from this statement; I am not sure that anybody really understands it.

Having a broad grasp of a wide variety of areas of knowledge should be the goal. Without it, politicians are at the mercy of pressure groups and the population as a whole are in no position to make decisions about a healthy lifestyle, to give just two examples.

At present, we have large sectors of society proclaiming that they know 'nothing scientific' as if they are proud of it. We also have physicists who know no biology and biologists who have no grasp of anything to do with physics. Both may know nothing of chemistry or biochemistry. In every case, the critical feature is to remember enough to put new information into its proper context. General awareness is important.

Generalised knowledge is best taught gently and patiently, making sure that the learner feels comfortable on the way. It is also critical that understanding, allied to knowledge, is reinforced over a substantial length of time. Merely 'covering' a subject will not do. Statistics, for example, are used all the time but the academic subject is often approached with an unnecessarily steep learning curve, making it unpopular and inaccessible to the majority.

A small number of people, relatively speaking, will choose to take a topic forward as a specialisation; they should be able to do so from a platform of generalised familiarity with a wide range of subjects: frameworks for future understanding.

Learning by rote

When I was at primary school we used to have regular sessions of chanting the 'times tables', with a great deal of repetition. I have often been grateful for the immediate recall of, for example, 9x7=63, without having to think or work it out. I suspect that the 'educationalists' wanted to get rid of rote learning at some point in the past, although my grandchildren still did their 'times tables'.

As long as the extent of rote learning is controlled, it retains a very useful function. There is nothing better than repetition for retaining useful information, although the format does not have to include chanting out loud. I would advocate rote learning to teach the relationship between fractions, decimals and percentages, for example.

We can think of rote learning, properly applied, as a seed for future understanding and development. Without a sense of number it is very hard to do maths or even to control your personal finances. In this way, strategically chosen rote learning contrasts profoundly with extreme breadth of relatively trivial factual information, as prevalent in some subjects.

The age of knowledge

It is difficult to pinpoint the exact period in history when people started to build a foundation of understanding of the world, supported by a unifying accumulation of knowledge. One reason that it is difficult is that the process started to be exponential, once information could be shared, quickly and at moderate cost. 'Exponential' in this context means that the quantity of available, accurate information has increased at an increasing rate as time has passed. We could say that the start of exponential growth was about the beginning of the 19th Century, as an approximation.

There are obviously newsworthy advances, associated with well known individuals such as Darwin and Einstein, but those who do not themselves carry out research will be unaware of the enormous amount of sound, well authenticated information that has accumulated and is still accumulating. To pick just one subject, if you go to any university library and look for 'Chemical Abstracts' you will find a series that started in about 1910 as a few thin volumes in the first year. At the time I retired, a year's output would occupy an entire shelf, even though printed on the thinnest paper available. That represented just the new knowledge accumulated in Chemistry in that year.

Up to the early 1900's it was possible to give students a reasonably comprehensive overview of their chosen subject in the space of a three year degree course. In the sciences, that has been impossible for perhaps 100 years. I recently looked at my 'O' Level notes in physics, dating back to the 1950's, and found a course that was entirely concerned with the history of the subject, very broad and very shallow. The 'scientific method' was not part of the curriculum. I could say the same about all the other subjects I was taught that had suffered from the same knowledge explosion. Obviously, that did not include languages or ancient history. Modern history has accumulated data in a more or less linear manner, not exponentially.

The enormous growth in factual knowledge, allied to the development of new research techniques, forces a reconsideration of the school curriculum. While the history of science is interesting, an understanding of some chosen areas is more important in the long run. The best approach may be to imitate the process of scientific discovery by presenting practical problems to stimulate the student's imagination. It is then necessary to come to terms with techniques as they are used, not just as historical accounts.

Breadth versus Depth

While on holiday recently I happened to pick up a book that had been brought by another guest. It was not the kind of book that I would normally read but I was startled at the level of agreement between the views expressed and those I hold myself, in subjects that are poles apart.

Under the title 'Lies my teacher told me' [James W. Loewen, Simon and Schuster, New York, 2007] the author explores in great detail the truth about North American history and contrasts the wealth of evidence with the descriptions prevalent in American text books. This is the major cause for his complaint but the part that I identified with came in the foreword.

James Loewen wrote

At year's end, no student can remember 840 main ideas, not to mention 890 terms and countless other factoids. So students and teachers fall back on one main idea: to memorise the terms for the test on that chapter, then forget them to clear the synapses for the next chapter.

This stratagem, to learn by heart with the intention to deliberately forget once the exam has passed, is incredibly damaging for the whole learning experience. It is bad enough to have to learn enormous wads of fact, but wiping the memory slate clean immediately after the exam says one thing: this whole experience is not part of the real world, it is a charade. Through my career I had the impression that the slate-wiping tendency was becoming more common among pharmacy students in the UK, to the point where it was deliberate. Students came from secondary school thinking that the stuff they were learning was just for passing exams.

It appears that a long period of knowledge gathering, getting faster exponentially, has resulted in some subjects, for example chemistry, having burst the boundaries. No longer is it possible to teach even a fraction of the available material in many (most?) subjects, including American history and the specialisations that are familiar to me.

It was a surprise to me, many years ago, that students in the first year of a university degree course could not answer simple, basic questions about the stuff they had been taught for 'A' Level Chemistry the year before. For a reader not familiar with the English system, 'A' Levels are the final school exams, used to judge a student's suitability for further study.

For most of the class, the material was totally unfamiliar. One young man, in a multiple choice test that included negative marking for wrong answers, scored -26%. When I checked, he had achieved an 'A' grade at 'A' level for the same subject just a few months before. I would have thought that he was having a laugh, but a number of others also scored negative marks.

Some years later, in another excellent university, I encountered another aspect of the same phenomenon.

Students were told that on my course there would be no regurgitation of facts and that they would be expected to understand the concepts and solve simple problems. Some came to me individually and expressed their concerns about having to understand the material. After sympathetic questioning, it became clear that these particular students had learned chemistry as a series of patterns without meaning, as if it was wallpaper.

For those with a basic understanding of chemical notation, the following example will clarify the situation :

The compound ethyl ethanoate, still sometimes called ethyl acetate, can be written in two ways

$CH_3COOCH_2CH_3$ or $CH_3CH_2OCOCH_3$

It gradually became apparent that the student would have learned one or the other and could not answer a question if the formula was written the other way round, exactly as if they were learning the pattern on a roll of wallpaper.

Initially I was astounded, but came to understand that it was neither the student's nor the teacher's fault. The syllabus was presented as a long series of facts, not as concepts to be understood and applied. The teachers had fulfilled their brief, to get the kids through the exam.

I should emphasise that these students adapted to the new environment and passed the course with ease. They were more capable than the system thought.

More recently I had the opportunity to read through a current 'A' level chemistry textbook. It was appalling. Just as James Loewen wrote about American history text books, 'A' level chemistry was presented as an enormous series of facts, to be learned parrot-fashion, with little attempt to explore the principles.

It is possible to start organic chemistry from a basis of fundamental mechanisms, which must be understood and retained. Once this is done, chemistry becomes orderly and comprehensible and it is possible to approach a previously unseen chemical reaction with confidence, making accurate predictions. This is what practising chemists do. When organised in this way chemistry becomes much more interesting.

Speaking before the second world war, Sir Ernest Rutherford is said to have expressed the view that in science 'there is just physics and stamp collecting'. If he did say this it must have been deliberately arrogant and offensive but at the time there was some truth in his perception. Organic chemistry, in particular, was presented as a series of recipes to permit the researcher to make a selection of old and new molecules. Many of these recipes were referenced by the names of the discoverers, such as the 'Bischler-Napieralski synthesis of isoquinolines' or the 'Skraup synthesis of quinolines'. There were hundreds of them.

When studying chemistry the student was expected to memorise a number of named reactions and potentially invent a synthesis based on them. It seems that the writers of chemistry textbooks, dominated by the syllabus, have scarcely moved on.

As a student, my entry to the chemistry profession was, to a large extent, influenced by Peter Sykes' little masterpiece *'A guidebook to mechanism in organic chemistry'*, first published by Longman in 1961. For the first time, the whole thing made sense, unlike the standard organic chemistry texts that were just reworking of the old recipe books. I still have a copy of the 4th edition, published in 1975, but I would say that the earlier versions are the best. Later versions tend to be too long, with too much detail. It is a tribute to Peter Sykes and an indication of the impact of his major work that there is now a 6th edition and it is still in print, 58 years later.

There is said to be an ancient Chinese saying:

I hear and I forget

I see and I remember

I do and I understand

In the UK, at least in some subject areas, we can now substitute

I read, learn and forget

Generally speaking, this is as far as it goes. Chemistry classes used to have demonstrations, which fulfil the 'I see and I remember' function but many demos are now considered too risky for Health and Safety. Sixty years after the classes, I can still remember some of the demonstrations that caught my attention. Chemistry used to be known as 'bangs and stinks' but experiments that produce either or both of these have been deleted. What a shame.

So far this has been largely negative but there are some positive lessons to be learned. In the first place, learning has to be based on some guiding principles, not on a mass of facts. The principles themselves have to be understood and soundly grasped. Once this part is secure, the learning process should be based on application of principles and repetition, in the same way that arithmetic used to be taught but with more inventiveness. In chemistry it is possible to repeat without being obviously identical: the mechanism can be the same but the molecule can be different.

While there may be cost limits to the amount of practical work that can be included, and recognising that practical work in its narrow sense may not be appropriate, it is perfectly possible to construct a course that involves solving problems, with emphasis on the plural. Repetition leads to understanding, confidence and retention.

Returning to the main theme, an education as proposed tends to encourage those who can only relate to a subject when they understand it, rather than learning disconnected facts.

Learning in depth rather than breadth requires a rethink of the fundamentals. At first sight it looks as though lots of good stuff is being neglected, not even mentioned. The decision to change requires a very clear vision of the potential benefits.

First, most of the students remember very little of the material that they have been required to learn if the scope is wide and there is no time for practice.

Second, the gain should not be simply in knowledge of disparate facts. As with primary school arithmetic, it is much more useful to leave with a set of skills than a vague idea. I remember a dear friend who taught maths in one of the best schools in Glasgow. Just before she left at the age of sixteen, a girl in her class, not one of the high fliers, came up to her and asked very quietly 'Please Miss, can you teach me sums?'.

On the same theme, my granddaughter was attending primary school when all the parents received a letter from the head teacher. Her recommendation was that all the parents who could afford the very low cost should enrol their children in a Japanese learning programme. Initially this only covered simple arithmetic and the work sheets were repetitive exercises such as 27+35 = ? There was page after page of this stuff, you would think really boring and perhaps it was, but the effect was to instil a feeling for numbers. The school recognised the value in this method but apparently was not allowed to use it.

Having a feel for something is important for confidence: in later years my granddaughter's acquired self belief gave her momentum and she passed 'A' level maths with an 'A' grade. Most people prefer to invest their energy when there is a prospect of success.

As a contrast, some years ago I bought five torch batteries in a shop on Glasgow's Argyle Street. They were 10p each and the shop assistant had to get her calculator to work out what I should pay. Quite possibly she could have done the sum in her head but had no confidence: automation and perhaps educational policy had robbed her of any feel for numbers.

In a different context, having no feel for the magnitude of numbers can lead to serious errors, when an obviously impossible answer is not recognised as such. In a pharmacy, such an error could kill a patient. At home, my wife and I have twice received gas bills that were an order of magnitude too high. In one case the employee who answered the phone could not see the problem.

An aspect of learning in depth that may be overlooked, in chemistry at least, is that repetition should extend over a prolonged period of time. Invariably, if you ask a student about something they did in earlier years you will provoke the alarmed response 'I think we may have done that last year'. The remedy is to bring topics back on a regular basis, so that it becomes part of the student's normal thinking, sometimes called 'internalised'. If the teachers do not adopt this approach they are conniving at a system that expects learning to be superficial and temporary. This is not the fault of the teachers, who invariably are teaching to a syllabus. The assumption, on the part of those who devise the syllabus, is that all past material is indelibly imprinted on the student's memory, despite the fleeting contact they have had and evidence to the contrary.

The mistake that has often been made when devising a syllabus is that it should be exciting. To the learner, excitement is a temporary sensation, a poor indicator of lasting involvement. Confidence in accomplishment is more powerful than sexy superficiality every time. There is enough transient content available to young people on TV and the internet, without extending it to the classroom.

When the learning process is reduced to a brief exposure to topics chosen for their entertainment value, we have reached rock bottom: this is little more than child minding.

Learning to swim

Think of a community that decides that teaching their ten-year-olds to swim would be a good idea; parents and schools agree. Common sense says that to do so requires a well-heated pool, since young children often carry little fat to protect them from cold water, and we want the kids to enjoy the experience. Assuming that a suitable pool exists nearby, we have to organise the teaching, which requires at least one suitable staff member. It would be unsafe to have very large groups, so we place a limit of twenty, knowing that fewer would be better.

The first group arrives at the pool on Monday and it is immediately apparent that some of the kids can already swim; they are transferred to another group with the same ability. Others in the class cannot swim but enjoy the warm water, while some are terrified of even getting their faces wet; it is essential that the children are treated as individuals. Those who are happy in the water can be encouraged to play, getting more confident as they do, before the next class on Wednesday.

The ones who are frightened of the water need special attention. Standing in the shallowest water, they will take more time before they start to explore their new environment. On Wednesday they will be less scared and the time after that even less. There is no rush.

Eventually, with two sessions every week, they will all gain confidence and the vast majority will become competent swimmers. Those who still cannot swim will at least be unafraid of the water and potentially able to learn to swim at some point in the future.

Alternatively, we could gather together in a class room and the kids could be taught the theoretical techniques of breaststroke, crawl and butterfly. They could learn the history of swimming, including the names of Olympic medal winners and those who have swum the English Channel, with the dates when they did it. Then they could have a written exam, with the results contributing to the school's OFSTED rating. That is the way we teach chemistry and a number of other subjects.

Aptitudes

Much of what follows is repetition of themes outlined elsewhere in this book. If this offends you, skip it; I am simply trying to express the same ideas in a slightly different way.

Although most people feel that they understand the word 'intelligent', it is very hard to provide a definition. Quiz programmes that carry the titles 'Mastermind', 'Eggheads' or even 'Brain of Britain' do not measure 'intelligence' but simply recall. 'University Challenge' requires not only recall but rapidity of response to the 'starter for ten'.

While a rapid, correct response to an obscure question about an ancient Greek myth or the Periodic Table of the Elements may be impressive, it does not imply intelligence, which for most people would require a certain level of organised thought. This does not matter for quiz shows that are purely for entertainment but, when judging a student's potential for higher education, tests of memory can be highly misleading. In many examinations, success comes from being able to think quickly and write quickly, quite unlike most of the situations that are encountered in real life.

For a very long time, academic potential in many subject areas has been measured by written examinations that are, for the most part, marked on the level of factual detail that is presented. In some subjects it is possible for a student to be awarded an 'A' grade, purely by learning answers to specific questions.

Maths is somewhat different, in that a natural way to test mathematical ability is by problem solving, but even here practice in mathematical techniques makes a huge difference. Much maths teaching is about acquiring familiarity with off-the-shelf means of solving problems, so that exam questions can be answered rapidly. Again, a good memory is valuable.

It would be ridiculous to propose that memory is unimportant, in any walk of life, for without memory we are not human; we have no social relationships and no basis on which to practise logical thinking. Unfortunately, the opposite is also true: without a capacity for in-depth analysis no amount of factual knowledge has any value.

The ability to recall immense detail is an **aptitude**. If that is what we call 'academic ability' we are throwing away most of the talent that is potentially available. Even the remarkable facility that some people have, for instant access to their memory banks, is of no avail when truly difficult problems present themselves. Albert Einstein would not have been a success on University Challenge, he needed time to think. 'Sorry, if you buzz you must answer straight away'.

'Aptitude' itself should not to be confused with instinct. It is possible for a child, without much apparent mathematical ability, to acquire confidence and hence 'aptitude' through repetition. With confidence comes a raft of social rewards; approval from the teacher and respect from fellow students, together with requests for help from the peer group that can add depth to the learning process for both. Confidence in one's own ability is vital when more difficult challenges are faced.

None of this addresses the more fundamental issue of 'book learning', the simple fact that a large proportion of the population do not respond to issues that are not, to them, real. Mankind developed in a world that had no paper; issues presented themselves in real time, in colour and in three dimensions. Many people, children included, will thrive in the real world but cannot take seriously a world which exists solely on paper. These people are not stupid, indeed some are potential innovators, capable of taking separate ideas and putting them together in ways that nobody had imagined. We can be confident that the bow-and-arrow was not invented by someone with a DPhil from Oxford University.

An educational process that in many areas is based on factual knowledge, acquired from text and other symbols written on paper, denies many people the chance of optimum intellectual development. This is society's loss, as well as a denial of opportunity to the individual. Work-based, hands-on learning will always be effective, provided that the conversation with the paper-based theorists is conducted on an equal footing. In some cases, hands-on learning can be profitably followed by 'book learning', once the student realises the significance of the task and is prepared to make the effort.

There is evidence that an aptitude for three-dimensional visualisation is more common for males than females. It is possible to rationalise this as an effect of Darwinian selection - males went hunting using spears - but in recent times very few do that. However, it may show up in a chemistry student's ability to visualise molecules in 3-D. Whether it matters in geometry, or plotting algebraic equations, is not at all clear. The significant angle to this is that students may benefit from flexibility in their studies, to choose what suits them, rather than being treated like sheep, as long as they have a broad grasp of all the vital areas.

If you were to take apart something complicated, like a motorcycle engine, most people would find it very difficult to reassemble. Some boys, and a few girls, would tackle the task with relish. This requires imagination, intelligence and 3-D visualisation, not properties tested by our exam system. In my view, it is the exam system that is wrong. It is damaging to the individual, who may be labelled as a failure in written tests, and it is a loss to the community, in failing to identify talent and provide opportunities for development.

The same applies to those whose basic aptitude is associated with physical strength and coordination. In a group of hunter-gatherers these attributes are highly prized and confer social status. In a classroom, sitting at a desk, they mean nothing. The result may be a loss of self-esteem and confidence, redeemed only by performance in games and sports. Loss of self-confidence does not help anybody, which means that those who are not academic need to be taught in non-academic ways. At the very least, a good footballer should be able to read, write and master sufficient number skills to survive in the modern world. Part of this lies in the ability to communicate: very often an apparent problem in understanding can be traced to language. Kids in the inner city tend to speak a language of their own, which cuts them off from much of mainstream society. They need to be bilingual in English and their own patois.

Wise versus clever

When I was young my mother liked to shop on Walthamstow market, in the open air. In the first hundred yards there were two barrow boys selling fruit. The first one was cheaper but often managed to conceal one bad apple in a bag of good ones. He was 'clever' or to use the current word, 'smart'.

The second barrow boy threw away the bad apples, so you could be sure of the quality of his fruit. Over the years his reliability paid off as his clientele expanded. He took a longer view and deserved to be called 'wise', though I doubt that anybody told him.

There is a tendency in modern Britain for those who are 'smart' to be admired, without distinguishing between the long and short views. I would say that Tony Blair was 'smart', in getting elected and becoming Prime Minister, but taking the UK into two long, damaging and expensive wars showed that he was not wise. He was also favourably disposed towards the opening of casinos, which bring in tax revenue (smart) at the expense of vulnerable gamblers (unwise).

Typically, the difference between 'wise' and 'smart' is one of superficiality. 'Smart' sees only the surface, immediate outcome. This difference is something that can be taught to children, although it may best be approached through games. Chess is a good example because the more you think ahead, the more likely you are to win. I doubt whether the average politician would choose chess before poker. Has anybody thought of including board games as part of mainstream education?

In general, the wiser person takes longer to make a decision. This may be taken as hesitancy or confusion, which is why the quick response is more impressive in the short term.

Curiosity

Most children have a natural curiosity about the world they live in, although the focus of their interest may be different. One child may be fascinated by the life in a pond, another may be more interested in stories about the ancient world.

Unfortunately, natural curiosity may be blunted by school teaching to the point where natural motivation is lost, in favour of a dull, obedient acceptance of society's demands, rewarded only by success in exams. While I would argue that there are certain basic skills that need to be compulsory, an insistence on learning solely for exams leads increasingly to the situation we have today, the learn-and-forget mentality.

Some people, the blessed ones, retain their natural curiosity throughout life. Even if they work in an office through the week, they may be involved with their local environment through a local or national organisation devoted to pond life. Alternatively, they may take part in discovering details of their local history. With curiosity as the driving force, any comparable activity can be life-enhancing. For some, this is the key to survival.

For someone who is fascinated by the discovery of Anglo-Saxon jewellery in a field it may be difficult to comprehend the devotion of others to the study of their local population of bats. To the casual observer both may be interesting, but the passionate commitment of the enthusiast to a narrow speciality is amazing. If we could retain that level of curiosity in school we would find that many more children would thrive, but we would probably have to re-think our whole approach, lock, stock and barrel.

Much of science is driven by curiosity, although for the professional there are other motivating factors. It is possible for curiosity to become obsession, which may become unproductive. On the other hand, an individual's perception may be important but not shared by the majority. If we are wise, we may choose to allow the off-piste researcher time to continue, rather than dictating what should and should not be studied.

In the past, the church decided what was truth and sometimes persecuted those who did not agree. We are now approaching an era in which 'big science' is trying to dictate what should be studied, a worrying parallel (see under 'Research Assessment Exercise').

Understanding

Different minds mean different things by 'understanding': a major difference is described under 'Physics'. For many people the trigger to understanding is to follow a train of logic, spelled out in detail at every step. I used this technique more or less instinctively for many years before I read that this was Socrates' method.

Essentially, before you can achieve illumination in someone's mind, you have to take the student back in small steps to a level that the student feels happy with. If this still doesn't do the trick, there is a gap that needs to be bridged. It is at this point that the teacher needs unlimited patience; any suggestion that you are losing your composure will lose the student's confidence in you. The fact that you have to go this far means that the learner is already embarrassed.

In my own teaching I sometimes had to go back in stages from the structure of morphine all the way to ammonia, before I could explain what happens to morphine in the body, as the pH varies. In a few cases I had to go right back to the molecular structure of ammonia. This process is not helped if the student has learned just to pass exams and then forgotten everything.

Once a state of enlightenment is reached, it is best to revisit the topic at intervals. With suitable reinforcement there is a good chance that the memory will persist.

I became convinced, over many years, that we have at least two forms of understanding. This may have been confirmed by studying brain activity, I do not know. The form that we are most familiar with is linked directly to speech and is used many times a day; for example, if I wish to tell you how to find the way to the post office. The second type of understanding is shared with animals that do not have the power of speech and it is important to realise that it is separate from instinct. It has a truly logical element.

As an example of the latter, there was a student in a problem-solving class who did the first three problems incredibly quickly. He simply 'saw' the answer and had some trouble in explaining how. Further on in the class he began to run into difficulty, as the problems became more complex and required organised speech-related thought.

Both routes to understanding are valuable, although for everyday purposes the speech-related process is more reliable, since it can be readily analysed and shared. But the more animalistic process should not be undervalued, because it is quicker and more direct. At times, more intuitive thoughts can find a way through when the common method fails. Having said this, the intuitive approach is not infallible and those who only access this way of thinking are likely to make big mistakes, 'jumping to conclusions'.

I tend to think that the really great thinkers use both ways to find an explanation. If the ideas come unexpectedly through the animal route it may take some time to justify the conclusion, since it does not come already written; much effort may be required to reach a conventional translation of what the thinker 'knows'.

Communication skills.

A significant aspect of the environment in a 'good' school is the development of an approach to speaking and writing that allows you to express your thoughts. In a fee-paying school there may be an emphasis on accent, such that your social class can be hidden (if necessary). This may be less common than it used to be.

For the majority, the essential feature is clarity. A non-essential feature is elegance, but even this carries advantages. English is an excellent language, more economical than many others in conveying ideas without ambiguity, but the decision to abandon style and grammar in favour of 'self expression' has led to a loss of clarity and often a total failure to understand the structure of the language.

I am conscious that Lynne Truss (Eats, shoots and leaves, published by Profile Books in 2003) has dealt with this topic in much greater detail and with greater elegance but in case you don't have a copy of her book to hand, the following will have to do.

A few examples:

'My uncle took my brother and I to watch a football match'

Presumably a teacher who did not understand grammar taught the kids to use 'I' instead of 'me'. Unless we are to abandon the use of 'cases', so that we need either 'I' or 'me' but not both, we should follow the rules. The sentence in question is an economical form of two sentences:

'My uncle took my brother to watch a football match'

and

'My uncle took <u>me</u> to watch a football match'

In the South-West of England, in years gone by, you might have heard

'My uncle took I to watch a football match'

but this form of speech has largely disappeared. The grammatically consistent sentence should be

'My uncle took my brother and <u>me</u> to watch a football match'

It is important to be consistent, but consistency without rules is difficult. We could argue that use of 'me' instead of 'I' in every context would be simpler, but compare these;

'Me and my brother went to watch a football match', which is frequently heard in modern English, with

'Me went to watch a football match', which you would never hear except possibly in the West Indies.

Another example (bear in mind that I did go to a grammar school and acquired a taste for accuracy as well as consistency):

The flavour of grapes depend on the kind of soil they were grown in.

This kind of error has become very common among journalists and TV presenters. In normal English, for a very long time, the sentence would have read

The flavour of grapes depends on the kind of soil they are grown in.

It is the flavour that depends on the soil. Another, consistent way of phrasing the sentence would be

With grapes, the flavour depends on the soil.

In my opinion, the clarity and elegance of a language are intimately connected to its internal consistency.

There is a tendency in the UK to adopt American pronunciation and spelling, which I find regrettable. Why replace the Anglo-Saxon word 'arse' with 'ass'? The latter is a donkey, for goodness sake. What on earth is an 'asshole' ? Maybe a donkey's arsehole?

Our abandonment of 'rude' words, where they could be identified, seems to have occurred in relatively recent times, when it was often linked to social class. The words themselves are not rude unless society deems them to be.

In the UK we have a lovely language, why not keep it and teach it?

Dialects

I treasure the way that people speak in different parts of the UK, even though it can make communication difficult. In the 1960's I would sometimes go to the pub before lunch on Sunday, with my father-in-law. He would have a lively conversation with a few old men who spoke broad Gloucestershire, a dialect that I followed with difficulty, to my embarrassment. Even so, I recall the way they spoke, with nostalgia; much of the conversation concerned their allotments and the health or otherwise of their vegetables. Today, it is possible to go to the same pub and hear strident conversations between relatively wealthy people from the London area, who have chosen to live in the countryside because the air is cleaner and there is less traffic.

There is still a Gloucestershire accent but it has been smoothed by TV and radio to be closer to mainstream (BBC) English. In the 21st Century most people from that county could work in London and be completely understood.

Go into a cafe in Devon now and there is a high probability that the staff will greet you with an accent that originates in the 'home' counties, around London. This will not be a 'posh' accent but quite unlike the way people spoke in the West Country fifty years ago. I regret this.

One of the joys of living in Glasgow has been to learn to understand what people say. Some of the words were strange to begin with and in broad Glaswegian the pronunciation can be very localised. Who in the South of England would understand 'Ra Juky Enbra' to mean the queen's husband?

The question for teachers is simple. Should classes be conducted in the local patois or should attempts be made to replace the local speech patterns with something more portable?

The answer, in my view, is that it should be both. Children going to school for the first time should if possible be welcomed in a dialect that is familiar. After that, if they wish to find employment elsewhere, they have to learn to moderate what they say. It is rather like learning to speak French if you go to live in France. Life is easier and more rewarding if you can communicate with people from as many different backgrounds as possible.

To go home at the end of the day and speak to your parents in their own language is essential, but if this language is not shared by future employers you will have to become bilingual. I had a friend at school who spoke standard Northeast London English at school. Crossing the threshold of his home, in what is now called Waltham Forest, he switched seamlessly into Glaswegian Scottish, the language of his mother and sister. At the time, I was baffled.

Dialects can be preserved, but it is vital, if we are to do so, that teachers and parents recognise the precious heritage that we have and do not attempt to confuse dialect with class. If we regard broad Gloucestershire as primitive, we shall lose it and end up all speaking in the same way. To some extent this is inevitable but I hope we don't end up speaking the language of the agricultural parts of the USA, which is an inelegant subset of English, perfect for cowboy films but not much else. I also think it odd that white teenagers are tending to pick up pronunciation and usage from Afro-English. I have been told that the following exchange between two white teenagers was overheard in Ipswich.

'Going to the party on Saturday?'

'I must aks ma bitch.'

'Aks' is not a typo.

Responsibility

In a system that takes young people into school and occupies much of their waking time for at least ten years, there is, or should be, a means of encouraging personal development. By itself, the emphasis on book learning tends to stunt all kinds of development, when parents and teachers only have eyes for exam results.

One way of making progress towards independence is to allow children to suffer the consequences of their failure to engage with reality. Many kids float along in a make-believe world where there is no penalty for behaving thoughtlessly. If your son likes playing football but is indifferent to the consequences if he does not remember his kit, let him go to school without it. When it comes to the afternoon he will look silly and next time may take responsibility himself. The alternative, as happens in most homes, is that his mother nags him constantly and he doesn't need to grow up.

Taking responsibility is a change of mental attitude that some find easier than others. It is far better for him to undergo the change gradually than to suddenly find that your 19-year-old son has maxed out on his credit cards and is deep in debt, pleading ignorance.

A small number of children have to take on the role of carer for a disabled parent. I am always impressed by their thoughtfulness and maturity when this happens. Although they are denied the carefree existence of their classmates, they are better equipped for life as adults. Having an 'old head on young shoulders' is rarely a bad thing. Ultimately, we all have to grow up, though rugby players seem to be able to postpone the process for many years.

Although fecklessness is not confined to boys and young men, it tends to be more common than with girls, who often take their mother as a role model. One way of gently pushing children towards maturity is to ask them to become part of the household rather than pseudo-aristocratic passengers. This means sharing chores as a matter of routine, not having to be bribed to do so. Even from an early age it may be possible to send a child to do some family shopping, for example. The earlier this happens, the more normal it seems to the child and is not a source of resentment. Children thrive when they are respected, as everybody does.

The hardest step towards independence, for a parent, is to allow a child to fail academically. A common consequence is that the child thinks of school work as being for his or her parents. At some point this has to change, whether the parent likes it or not; you cannot follow behind your child through adulthood. This thought connects with the comments under 'Learning later in life', that a child who is late growing up, or fails to find his or her niche, may benefit from adult education. There is often a kind of panic about making life choices at the time that the school curriculum dictates, rather than when the person is ready. In reality, you can have a break for several years and come back to learning with far better prospects than opting for something with no enthusiasm, simply because your exam grades were better in that subject.

Another thought in passing: if we could get away from the sausage machine approach to education, we might envisage mixed-age classes, where some of the students are strongly motivated. Attitudes tend to be infectious.

Discipline

In the developed world, society has moved away from imposed discipline; for some it is a dirty word. We often have a view of those who refuse to knuckle under as admirable rebels. Sometimes I share that view but there is a curious dichotomy between imposed and voluntary discipline. The Rolling Stones were the bad boys of popular culture, frequently indulging in risky behaviour, but listen to the band when they play together and they exhibit very tight discipline. Their highly structured sound requires the acceptance of rhythm, harmony and coordination as finely honed as any symphony orchestra.

The difference is an understanding that some mutually acceptable control is required. Boys who behave badly in class may listen carefully to the coach when playing football, (though what he says has to make sense), and do their best to fulfil the team's requirements.

Some parents do not understand that any social group, human or animal, requires some loss of freedom in return for the benefits that cooperation brings. Their children tend to be wild and destructive, eventually banned from normal schools and with an increased probability of turning to crime. I have no easy solution but the spectrum of bad behaviour is a continuum, from mild rebelliousness to psychosis. Those who are just a little difficult may be more imaginative and possibly more intelligent than the average, which makes them less likely to accept assertions that do not appear to make sense. These kids require to be taught with more sensitivity; often they will repay that sensitivity in a way that dull obedience will never do.

In marked contrast, groups of children without discipline or self-control may become feral. A recent example in the UK was a group vandalising a car outside the owner's home. When he tried to stop them, they killed him. For children like this, society has to be firm and punishment has to be severe. Most importantly, the environment has to be one in which punishment is understood and enforced without fail. Too often, the theorists propose subtlety when the kids themselves only respect the old biblical concept of 'a tooth for a tooth'. There is room for some imagination in devising effective punishment, in an era when prison may be regarded as a welcome, safe refuge from violence on the streets.

This is not a time to reduce the size of the police force. If some of our politicians were made to spend regular periods living on inner city housing estates they might change their attitude to policing.

Practical skills

At one time, the next generation of plumbers would come from the previous generation by learning on the job with their fathers. With the perception that any course at a university is a higher status option, the UK lost a substantial proportion of its plumbers. The lads and lasses who might have filled the vacancies are instead, after graduation, pulling pints in the local night club. The plumbers who came to fill the gaps are from Eastern Europe, primarily Poland.

It may be assumed that current shortages of trained manpower in the manufacturing industries can be traced to the same perception that social status is more important than earning power. If a very large proportion of the potential workforce is going to university to follow courses that involve no practical skills, we should expect a high level of graduate unemployment or at least menial employment in unskilled occupations.

I asked for permission to quote from Alexander McCall Smith's book 'Bertie's guide to life and mothers' but this was not forthcoming, which is a pity because his elegant phrasing is far better than mine. With gentle mockery he discusses the possible extra attributes that 'classicists' and art historians might bring to their employment in coffee bars, perhaps discussing the 'Florentine renaissance' as they hand over the chosen beverage. At the time of writing there are acute shortages of butchers and HGV drivers, which leads me to wonder if there might be degrees in History of Art with joint honours in butchery or driving trucks.

Much of the attitude to class arises from the dismissive treatment of so-called 'blue-collar' workers by those who perceive themselves to be of higher status, as in the Bristol paint factory (see under 'Management'). Unless we can tackle class issues in society generally, we shall never be competitive as a nation. In the USA class is defined by wealth, which itself can be damaging, but at least it is not based on ancient perceptions derived from the landed aristocracy. It is curious that mankind, as with other social animals, has to have a pecking order.

Learning in school

A philosophical conundrum

Although we value freedom above many things, we have decided across the developed world that it is acceptable to confine our young people to classrooms from the age of five or six, five days a week, for at least ten years.

Very few of them would choose this way to spend their time. If we think back, maybe two hundred years or less, learning started even before the age it does now but not in a classroom. If the parents worked on the land, the learning experience would occur in the open air. Most importantly, learning would take place alongside a parent and would be focussed on practical matters. In a more urban environment there was a high chance that the son of a joiner would become a joiner, with a practical introduction at an early age. There would be little or no 'book learning'.

With mechanisation on the land and a rapidly growing population there was mass migration to the cities, where the chance of finding the same work as your parents was remote. With widespread poverty it was necessary to find whatever work you could and life expectancy was very short. The figure quoted for Manchester in the early 1800's was seventeen; in Liverpool it was nineteen.

Under these circumstances it was highly beneficial to learn to read and write and master arithmetic. School teachers were paid, not very well, but they could live better than the majority and they were respected for their ability. Schoolchildren tended to be obedient and feared their parents if they misbehaved. Discipline was rarely a problem but when required was maintained through direct punishment, often physical.

The same principles persisted through most of the twentieth century, until more enlightened attitudes prevailed. Unfortunately, without the threat of physical punishment but with strict rules about attendance, some children started to misbehave. Society still hasn't found a way to deal with this situation.

An over-riding consideration in modern society is the expectation that women will work to earn money. This cannot be reversed in any way that women would find acceptable, so somebody has to look after the kids. This role has fallen to school teachers. To make the confinement in class more acceptable, the teachers have been instructed to broaden the curriculum and make it more entertaining. Unfortunately this has led to the loss of much that was worthwhile and given the whole experience an air of unreality.

In earlier times, children were used in ways that we would now find horrific. The classic example is of boys being sent up chimneys to clean them, but stories from the so-called mills used to produce cloth were almost as bad, with young children being expected to work for twelve hours a day, without protection from dust, noise and machinery.

As a result, children in cities are today not expected to work at all, except sometimes to deliver newspapers. This has not been thought through. On farms, the children often do useful work with animals, for example delivering lambs and looking after them. The effect is beneficial in many ways: the child feels valued and becomes accustomed to the idea that they should work. They earn respect and become closer to their parents. Not least, they learn skills that will become useful in adulthood.

In 'primitive' societies children are absorbed into the life of the community as soon as they are physically capable. Work is expected and natural; it is also clearly essential to their peers and elders.

When children grow up in cities they have no idea what they are going to do later in life. Any value in employment, other than pay, may be invisible, and sometimes the sheer drudgery of modern industrial practice will be resented. When a modern mother refers to her daughter as 'my princess' she is contributing to a situation in which her daughter does not expect to work or even to help around the house.

Parents

Primary school teachers in the UK have recently been complaining that kids have been starting school without being potty trained. This is an extension of recent parental attitudes to other responsibilities. Broadly speaking, a majority of parents are convinced that their skills and experience do not permit them to make a contribution to their children's education. In some cases it may be laziness, in others lack of confidence. The situation is not helped by educational theorists, who change things like the methods to add and subtract numbers, so the parents do not understand.

Ideally, parents need to be included in the educational process, not just informed about their child's progress. They can start by preparing their children before school, to be accepting of parental authority in the home. A recent TV programme explored the possibility that children could be trained like dogs, which sounds dreadful. In practice the approach is very sympathetic to the child's needs, as it has to be with a dog. The emphasis is always on positive reinforcement of good behaviour. This is not the place for a detailed description but if you have a child that is likely to 'throw a wobbler' for no apparent reason it would be worth investigating.

In more deprived areas, it is more likely that parents will be unable to help. In some cases they may be dismissive of the value of education, which in their experience is lacking in relevance. Others may be unable to read or write. In a recent survey, it was stated that more than five million UK adults were only marginally literate, able to understand simple texts but no more. Five million!

An approach that concentrates on adding survival skills rather than ethereal factoids may be more appealing to the parents, who could be invited to attend classes with their children, for example in learning to manage their money and avoid the loan sharks. This might also be a way of keeping control of an unruly class. I would define a factoid as an item of information that is useless, irrelevant and quite possibly wrong.

Punishment

Educational theorists have been arguing for decades that punishment has no place in learning or in controlling behaviour. In contrast, studies of social animals show that punishment plays a significant role in group dynamics, specifically to allow the group to function as an entity, when appropriate, rather than as individuals.

Jane Goodall tells a story about the Gombe Stream chimpanzees, relaxing in the heat of the afternoon. One young male was swinging from a branch and touching a male baboon who was relaxing with his troupe, near the chimpanzees. The youngster kept doing this until the baboon had had enough and retaliated, but not very aggressively. When the youngster cried out, one of the male chimps woke up and smacked the baboon.

Once order was re-established, the young chimp started again, swinging back and forth to nudge the baboon and provoke a response. When the baboon again did so and he cried out once more, the big male chimp smacked the young chimp.

In a wolf pack, the alpha male and female keep order by domination; they punish behaviour that they find unacceptable by growling, showing their teeth and if necessary biting. Discipline is maintained by common assent until such time as the alpha pair are losing authority through injury or old age. Lion prides have some similar behaviour patterns, as do hyenas and even meerkats. It is very important that punishment is instant, so that the transgressor knows what caused the problem.

Nobody would suggest that human beings should maintain social order in the same way that wolves do, but some means of control is highly beneficial. The alternative is for the children to run wild, causing problems for everybody, including themselves.

Physical punishment can be effective, used sparingly, but can become a habit. It is far better to use other methods but to do so requires patience and insight, both of which may be lacking in some families. When training a dog, the desired behaviour is rewarded at frequent intervals and it does not take very long before the dog behaves as the owner dictates. For the dog to recognise its own inferior status in the owner's home is vital: a dominant dog is a nightmare.

Once the pecking order is established, both owner and dog are happy; it is not cruel to require obedience, because the wolf pack operates in the same way.

A similar approach applies to children. A sense of security comes with accepting their parent's authority and once this pattern is established it is easy to reward good behaviour. The contrary is also true and new parents may be surprised at the determination that some small children may show, to dominate. As with a dog, this must not be permitted, for reasons that I hope are obvious.

As with dogs, most children can learn to respond to spoken commands and as the child grows the complexity of the concepts they understand will increase. In this way it is possible to establish a mutual understanding that is rewarding for parent and child.

If the parents wish their child to be accepted at school it is vital that responsive patterns of behaviour be established at an early stage, before the child goes to school. For school teachers to control an unruly child, in the presence of a number of other children, may be impossible. It is a nightmare for the teacher and does the child no favours.

If a situation is reached in which the whole class is uncontrollable, there must be simple, effective measures to remove the wild ones. The alternative is to abandon all hope of education. At this point a dog would either be put down or taken to an expert for training. The former is not a remedy for humans but there must be ways that wild children can be retrained, using the same principles. The trainers have to be strong-minded and capable of choosing when to reward and when to punish. It should be appreciated that punishment does not have to be physical; well-chosen words from a respected adult may be enough but the respect has first to be earned.

Freedom is not unlimited; even in a group of hunter-gatherers there will be rules and as a social system becomes overcrowded the rules become more complex and more numerous. There is no universal rule for the use of punishment as a tool in controlling behaviour. In a rough inner city environment there may be a need for tough action that would be totally wrong in a country village. There is no way to decide on an effective punishment without knowing the circumstances. Withdrawal of a privilege is one possibility but this depends absolutely on the nature of the relationship.

Many problems would be avoided if parents attended classes before the child is born. In the days before World War II, when very large families were normal, the older children would assist their parents in training their younger siblings to behave. In so doing they learned how to control children in advance of the time when they would have their own.

Learning later in life

One of the problems with the traditional approach to schooling is that the young enter a pipe at the age of four or five and come blinking into the daylight when they are in their late teens, very often antagonistic to learning. Some time later they may have cause to revise their thinking, having discovered something that they can relate to. The Open University may help in the UK but the decision to re-enter education is difficult; it requires a change of lifestyle and some awkward choices about finance, for example.

A different kind of structure would permit re-entry at any age but first it would be helpful to abandon the pipeline concept of education. To repeat the message, we waste a lot of talent, partly owing to the excessive use of academic fact-based learning and partly because, as some humourist once remarked, education is wasted on the young.

In a career of about forty years, I occasionally had the pleasure of teaching people who came to my subject a little later in life. Sometimes they had gone through the pipe line and completed a degree in a subject that ultimately did not satisfy them. Others may have come out of the pipe line after school and refused to follow their teacher's advice to continue in full-time education. In both cases, these people were a pleasure to teach. They worked at the subject because they wanted to, not because it was expected.

There is a big difference in the rate that men and women mature. I have often observed that 'A girl of 18 is a woman but a man of 18 is a boy'. This has far-reaching implications. In our educational process, entry to university is governed by 'A' level results in England, or 'Highers' in Scotland. The girls, across the board, get better results than the boys, so any course at university that has competitive entry tends to have a preponderance of women.

In my lifetime, the percentage of undergraduates enrolled on law degree courses has changed from less than 10% women to more than 50%.

So what? In the health professions, for example, female graduates tend to marry other health professionals. After a few years they have children and most stop working full time. In a 1996 survey conducted by the Royal Pharmaceutical Society, of female pharmacists in the 30-35 age group only 18% worked full time. The figure for men was 79%.

You might think that older women would have worked longer hours as their children grew up and left home, but there was only a slight tendency to do so. The outcome was a shortage of pharmacists, despite increasing intakes to the schools of pharmacy and the opening of a number of new schools.

Put bluntly, on average a male pharmacist returns more value in working hours for his education than a female, over his lifetime. Nobody would suggest that entry to the professions should be barred to women, but an approach to teaching that made life more stimulating at school level might help to encourage the boys to work harder. Alternatively, it could be made more normal for men or women to enter a profession at a later stage in their life. At present, we have very low expectations of flexibility.

Exercise and the school week

Given freedom, the vast majority of children will play games that involve a lot of running around. It is only in recent years that parents have acquired an image of the world outside as one full of murderous paedophiles. With the invention of electronic games it is possible for children to play by themselves in 'safety', without leaving the house.

The result is an epidemic of obesity and a widespread loss of communication skills. Some children are having to be taught how to speak when they go to school!

Typically, schools have limited the children to one games afternoon in the week. The rest of the time has been confined to the classroom, learning 'stuff' to pass exams. Success for teachers and the school has been to climb the league tables, based on exam pass rates. As well as being overly academic, with negligible weight placed on practical skills, the material tested in exams does not stay with the children. With the exception of those with unusually retentive memories, stuff learned in the first year cannot be recalled even in the second year.

Some children hate exercise, for whatever reason: they may be short-sighted or they may be poorly coordinated. For the majority, some will relish contact sports like rugby while others will prefer athletics or tennis. Common sense dictates that they should be allowed to choose, provided that there are facilities available. Selling off the school playing fields was never a good idea.

The way that activities are planned is important. I suspect that most schools are more enlightened than mine, in the 1950's. In breaks and at lunch time we played with lightweight plastic footballs but on one afternoon a week in the winter we had organised football, played with old leather balls with rough surfaces. The balls were very heavy, particularly in wet weather, and 'house games' would see 22 twelve year olds unable to kick the ball more than 20 yards. The ball made tiny movements, propelled by undeveloped muscles, first in one direction and then the other until a goal was scored. At any time, apart from the goalkeepers, most of the players could be found within a few yards of the ball.

Nobody was excused, so a few unfortunates who had no wish to be there would stand around shivering, getting no exercise at all. It never occurred to the teachers to allow us to play with the plastic balls that we used at lunchtime.

Children develop at different rates. Some boys get an early testosterone boost and acquire muscles that others can only hope for. The difference in physical power is enormous. Trying to play team games when selection relies on age rather than physique is hopeless.

There is no simple solution to these problems but some progress could be made if we got away from the idea that the whole week should be spent on academic study. This is a revolutionary suggestion for the state sector in the UK but is logical if we accept that our present system of 'listen, learn and forget' achieves virtually nothing.

For simplicity, imagine a school day that starts with some in-depth study, based on an activity that the children can master and that has relevance to their futures. Such an activity will be revisited at intervals throughout their time at school, so that familiarity is reinforced. Practical activities, such as woodwork or building electronic circuits, will be included whenever appropriate.

In the afternoon there could be freedom under supervision! If some of the boys or girls want to play football, let them do so and let them organise it for themselves. If some of them want to do needlework, let them do so. If others wish to sit quietly reading, why not let them? Some thought has to be given to programmes of exercise that can be followed by unfit children, probably short in duration, possibly indoors and certainly not standing around in cold weather.

It would be presumptuous to attempt to lay out a complete curriculum based on the above. The ideas are presented as a remedy for some of the problems that children have with school at the time of writing; obesity, boredom and rejection of the totality of education.

The major obstacle is the exam structure, an iron-clad edifice that dictates everything that schools have to do. Without a recognition that phantom learning is a waste of time there can be no improvement. By 'phantom learning' I mean the current practice of teaching to a syllabus that is stuffed with facts, to be memorised just long enough to pass the next exam. One university vice-chancellor used to refer to the 'tyranny of examinations' and he was right, though powerless to change the system.

James Hilton, the author of 'Goodbye Mr Chips' and a range of other novels as well as film scripts, attended my old school, in Walthamstow, about thirty years earlier than I did. The school had moved premises in that time but apparently not much else had changed. As a sequel to his most popular work he wrote 'To you, Mr Chips', first published in 1938 by Hodder and Stoughton.

The book starts with 'A chapter of autobiography', which includes the following:

.... it has often struck me as remarkable that an age that restricts the hours of child-employment in industry should permit the much harder routine of schoolwork by day and homework in the evenings. A twelve-hour shift is no less harmful for a boy or girl because it is spent over books.

The chief reason for such slavery is probably the life-and-death struggle for examination distinctions in which most schools are compelled to take part.

Food

I use this title rather than 'cookery' because much healthy food does not need to be cooked. It is welcome that cookery classes are now a feature for boys as well as girls but they tend to skim the surface; since they do not form part of the academic priority system they do not get much time or importance allocated to them.

At one time, girls were taught to cook by their mothers. This essential life skill has been lost in many families, for reasons that are quite complicated, but we know that the educational process was not academic in approach. It was deadly serious and would normally involve a limited repertoire of dishes.

As with any learning, repetition is essential. Why not organise the classes so that the children eat their own produce? If this were normal practice a failure to prepare edible food could result in further attempts until success was achieved. It would be anticipated that first-time success would become more common and the children would leave school with a useful skill.

Much of the attitude to the preparation of food is tied up with the expectation of success. If the cook is confident, the energy barrier is much lower. Who wants to spend time in the kitchen when the result may be inedible?

Is the ability to make your own healthy food really less important than the average content of the typical academic syllabus? Perhaps the 'upper class' normally eat in restaurants or employ their own cooks but this should not impact on those with less money.

Hygiene and food are closely linked. The necessity for a cook to be hygienic is common sense and should be linked to other food skills. It is a waste of time to teach biology as an academic subject, to be learned, examined and forgotten, when it can be linked to simple survival. While it may not be significant to be able to label the parts of a dissected earthworm, knowing what causes disease is important. It is equally important to know how bacteria differ in their susceptibility to bactericides and how misuse of antibiotics can lead to the development of resistance. We should all know how bacteria thrive in badly prepared or badly stored food. On a broader theme, we should all know how fungi contribute to the environment and when they can be dangerous.

As with all the topics discussed in these pages, it is no good teaching microbiology in one short block and expecting the average child to carry that knowledge through the life that follows. Every subject needs to be revisited on a regular basis.

The correct way to feed very young children should be part of everyone's school experience, not as an academic study but for purely practical reasons. Poor nutrition can arise from poverty, which is a separate issue, but unbalanced, unhealthy feeding of infants should be avoided by education well before parenthood. As ever, this must not be a fleeting exposure but internalised through repetition. Failure to do so lays the basis for a variety of health problems in later life and a massive load on the National Health Service. I have seen a child in a pushchair drinking through a teat attached to a bottle of Irn Bru.

Learning in universities

University funding

When I started as a university teacher in 1970, there were relatively few universities and it was possible for the government to support them by means of block grants. In this system, a sum of money was provided annually and the university could spend it as the senior officers deemed fit.

Under this system there was no necessity for a quota of successful graduates from any particular cohort of students. In some years the students stimulated and supported each other to work hard, with excellent exam results across the board. The next intake might include a small number of charismatic people who thought that working hard was not for them. When this happened quite a few might fail or graduate with poor degrees. The authority of the department was not questioned as long as the external examiner agreed with the marks allocated.

At some point in the late 1970's there were large numbers of people out of work and it occurred to the politicians that it might be possible to keep them in education for a few more years, to make the statistics look better. To make a sufficient difference the number of universities needed to be greatly increased, which would cost a lot of money.

Up to this point a school-leaver who was accepted by a university would receive financial support from the state. A huge increase in numbers would make this unaffordable so a scheme was implemented that covered all aspects.

First, the block grant system was abandoned. In future all universities would be paid on a head count; more students enrolled would mean more money. Once enrolled, the income would continue as long as the student remained on board.

Second, in England and Wales the students would have to pay fees, a proposal that was rejected in Scotland.

Superficially, the scheme worked. Families that had never seen a member go to university were delighted at the improvement in status that their child represented. Teachers regarded progress to university as the benchmark of success, irrespective of the nature of the course being followed and the employability of graduates. For the politicians, there was a gratifying fall in the number of unemployed.

In reality, the new universities found attracting school leavers to be a challenge. Their solution was to invent courses that were cheap to run and superficially attractive. 'Media studies' became common, 'surfing' was only possible for a seaside institution. Go through the subjects seeking recruits in late summer through the clearing system and you will find many more.

In some places more expensive degrees such as chemistry were abandoned.

The worst effects of the changes concern the necessity to keep 'bums on seats'. With widened access, more students who were not academically minded found themselves at university. It should be understood that these young people were not necessarily unintelligent, they simply had never been attracted to abstract study for its own sake. As a result, they were poorly motivated and had poor exam marks but the system was designed to keep them off the unemployment register, so they could not be failed.

For many years I was external examiner in a wide range of institutions of varying maturity, all of which had to adjust their expectations of student performance. Typically this meant fewer fails and a huge increase in the number of first and upper second class degrees awarded. Fee paying students would tend to choose a university that awarded lots of 'good' degrees, apparently.

When it became clear that many of the newly invented courses did not improve the graduate's employment prospects, there were concerns that the numbers would go down. To counter this, it was put about that over all courses the salaries of graduates were better than those of non-graduates. It was not pointed out that graduates in the professions such as medicine, dentistry, veterinary science and law were skewing the data. If you were to survey the prospects for those with degrees in the newly invented subjects, many of whom have few saleable skills, the results would be expected to be different.

I am sure that the motives behind the changes to university funding were not entirely concerned with reducing the number of unemployed school leavers. There seems to have been an impression that academic tertiary education is always valuable and should be made more widely available. Unfortunately, the employment prospects for a graduate are at least partly based on the reputation of the university and the difficulty of gaining a place to study there, as well as the area of study.

The decision to rename technical colleges as universities reflects class attitudes to applied subjects, specifically among politicians. To secure the best outcome for the UK we need decision-makers who will encourage the young to pursue careers in subjects that make them capable of earning a living, without giving them the false impression that they are lower class. Quite simply, persuading a young person that he or she should read for a BA in history, when their aptitude is for practicality, is a disaster.

Being an academic

An academic is someone who enjoys studying something for its own sake. Curiosity is a major factor. This is primarily a search for understanding and can range from the behaviour of monkeys in a rain forest to the properties of numbers.

If you only feel able to give your full attention to something with immediate significance, you may find a home in a university but you may be better off in an environment that is dedicated to more applied study.

Either way, it is far better to be a round peg in a round hole. In my experience, a very small proportion of the population are truly academic, maybe as few as 2%. Choosing an academic career because you think, or are told, that it is superior to study and think in an abstract context, may be a mistake.

A practically-minded student may prosper in an environment where problems are encountered in practical situations but the same student may struggle on an academic course that seems to bear no relationship to everyday life. Practical problems may be encountered or simulated in a university but the best place may be a working environment where the problems are real, immediate and genuinely important.

It is worth acknowledging that universities may be better at keeping abreast of technical developments than industrial companies, simply because they have the time to do it, so close relationships are likely to benefit both. In this context, a small new local university may be more appropriate than an enormously prestigious but profoundly academic provider.

A young person who is persuaded to follow a paper-based university course rather than an apprenticeship should be certain that he or she is academic in outlook. Even then, it might be better to follow a course that leads to well-paid employment; you can always study Etruscan pottery in your spare time.

The class system

Unlike European countries that had permanent revolutions, Britain retained its ancient aristocracy and the associated class attitudes. The concepts of 'middle class' and 'working class' are still current in 21st Century Britain. It would be understood that a window cleaner is working class but a bank manager is middle class, even though both work for a living. Although the landed gentry are reduced in number, a new aristocracy has arisen based on wealth acquired through other means. This was primarily through manufacturing and now by manipulating money in the banking system.

Unlike France and Germany, where engineering is hugely respected - the French word for an engineer is 'ingenieur' as in 'ingenious '- the British establishment retained a contempt for those who get their hands dirty. To them, the engineer was somebody who oiled the engine and kept it running.

When I took the 11-plus in 1955, there were three possible outcomes. If I scored high marks I would go to the grammar school, less high marks and I would be sent to the local technical college. Failing that I would go to the secondary modern and do woodwork. The significant aspect of this system is that the academic grammar school was rated most highly. In my own (Grammar) school the 'arts' subjects, principally languages and history, were reasonably well taught, as was maths if you could get past 'O' level. The sciences were rather hit-and-miss affairs and there was absolutely no route to any kind of engineering.

Turning now to the ancient universities, until well into the 20th Century Oxford did not teach English, though the dead languages Latin and Ancient Greek were revered. Chemistry, hugely important to Britain's prosperity, was taught in Manchester, as it was in Germany, for many years before Oxford joined in. The first Oxford chair in engineering was appointed in 1908 but the university did not seem to recognise its proper place until the 1950's. Pharmacy is still not taught in any of our ancient universities, though it is vitally important to the health of the community and is a perfectly respectable academic discipline.

Ancient attitudes to class persist even to this day. 'Public' schools exist to give the wealthy an advantage, charging high prices to ensure favourable staff/student ratios and well motivated teachers. Attendance at one of the schools charging high fees confers a better chance of entry to a prestigious university, with the opportunity to make life-long relationships with future pillars of the establishment. In the UK an Oxford degree makes a career in politics more likely, even if your degree is in a non-technical subject like history. How many countries would trust their economy to a graduate with a degree in history and no evidence of numeracy?

Continuing this theme in the context of survival in a difficult world, the performance of the British upper crust in guiding the economy has been woeful. Decisions tend to be made along guidelines established by the legal profession, who make no secret of their basic principle that future actions should be based on who wins the argument and not on the search for truth. This approach is nowhere more apparent than in the arguments about climate change, where governments make compromises. Climate change is real and deadly; you cannot bargain it away or postpone the consequences by argument. Polish coal miners will lose their jobs but in years to come they will see that the alternatives are too awful to contemplate.

For the survival of the UK as a place where rational decisions are made, children need to be educated in matters of significance, not ancient Greek fairy stories, especially when their social background gives them a head start in becoming influential politicians. Some of the education of a politician needs to be in the community, doing work of the kind that the vast majority have to do. Taking young men from public school into Oxford University and then directly into politics is a recipe for disaster.

Let us face facts. The curriculum that was established in the middle ages, when few things were understood about life, the universe or anything, was based on the writings of a few people, mostly men, from 1000 to 3000 years before. To continue with this in the 21st Century is ridiculous. Before a schoolboy or girl chooses 'arts' subjects there should be a clear understanding of what this means for their future career. With few exceptions, the chosen speciality will lead to difficulty in finding employment. At the time of writing, the 'arts' graduate in England will also be saddled with a debt that will be difficult to repay without further training in something more applicable.

All of this means that the traditional division in schools into those following 'arts' or 'science' should be abandoned. Although 'arts' departments in universities are cheap to run, since they do not require laboratories or much in the way of equipment, we should ask the question 'If the graduate is unemployable after three years study, is this an economic option?' Perhaps 'arts' degrees are actually rather expensive.

This comment is not confined to the 'arts'. It may also be difficult for a science graduate to find the kind of work that they would prefer. We should expect that such a graduate would at least be numerate but their communication skills may be lacking. Whether 'arts' or 'sciences', it would be helpful if higher education institutions were prepared to take some interest in the employability of their graduates and modify their teaching accordingly. This is particularly important when undergraduates are regarded as paying customers.

The Research Assessment Exercise

Few people outside universities will have heard of this but it has had a drastic effect on the quality of life for teaching staff.

With the decision to change the basis for university funding (see under 'Learning in Universities') came the realisation that there was insufficient money to pay dozens of new universities for them to support research as well as teaching. Up to this point, a university teacher who was not ambitious, or was simply running out of energy as he or she got older, could opt for a life of teaching. In some cases this meant that they could concentrate on writing books and improving their communication skills. In other instances it meant that they had long holidays and a very privileged life style, irrespective of the age of the institution. Imagine if you were teaching at one of our ancient universities, with three eight-week terms a year and no responsibilities for the remainder of your time.

To allow the funding system to be changed, a small group of self-styled elite universities proposed the Research Assessment Exercise. This would apply to all subjects in all universities and would take place every four years, for a limited period. There were some unanticipated consequences that I will come to shortly.

The initial idea was that universities would be graded on a scale of 1 to 5 for research, based on two measures. First, a count of published papers for the previous four years and second, the amount of research money brought in over the same time. The concept envisaged an evolutionary approach, in which universities that were less well rated for research would receive smaller allotments of central resource and would decline over time, eventually giving up all ambition except in teaching.

In the grand scheme there would be good universities, funded for teaching and research, and teaching-only universities that would get much less money. Unfortunately, as one of the architects of the scheme explained to me, there were awkward places like Dundee University which had a world-class biochemistry department but not much else (his words, not mine; I am sure that Dundee had many other good people).

Their second thought was that good departments, in otherwise ordinary universities, would have to move. They would have to do so if they wished to retain funding. This suggestion was abandoned soon after it was started, once they realised how many good departments there were in the smaller universities and the impossibility of thousands of members of staff, many with children at school, being forced to uproot and go elsewhere.

The RAE started in the 1980's, based on the publications and research income of individual departments rather than whole universities. In chemistry there was a certainty, on the part of those who had devised the scheme, that Oxford and Cambridge would come out top. Imagine their dismay when the top chemistry department turned out to be Salford! This was not just unintended, it was not permissible, so the rules were changed retrospectively. Rather than counting total research income, only income from recognised research councils would count. Salford's problem was that they had a lot of industrial money: you might think that this was exactly what the country needed to keep its manufacturing businesses working to the best effect, maintaining employment and profits as well as returning tax to the treasury. But no, not if it meant threatening Oxford and Cambridge.

No doubt the government realised the problem and challenged Oxbridge to be more industry-friendly, which forced the dons from the dreaming spires to change their ways, up to a point, but whether their hearts were in it is doubtful. One Oxford professor would accept industrial funding very readily but would never participate in industrial research, leaving that task to junior employees.

At the outset, the RAE was meant to run for very few four-year cycles. It is an expensive and time-consuming process, but more than thirty years later something similar is still operating. I may be wrong but I don't think that any other country has followed the UK's lead. The whole purpose was to maintain an academic class system, in which a group of self-selected elite universities would remain unchallenged by upstarts.

There are other problems with this system. An old concept of a university was as a place in which people could study together, learning from each other. Research was inseparable from teaching.

Another problem arises from the source of teaching staff for the new underclass of teaching-only institutions. Many candidates for employment, strongly motivated to follow their own discipline, would not be prepared to take a job which is teaching-only. Their resilience is the reason why the exercises continue.

The biggest problem is not obvious at first sight but could be the most important, potentially devastating for Britain's future. History teaches that the most original thinking tends to come from unexpected sources. Major institutions tend to think that they are untouchable, when in practice they tend to acquire a routine pattern of thought. Even world-class research facilities tend to get stuck in a rut.

They become very good at certain things, making steady progress, but will not make the giant leap of imagination that takes mankind into a new era. It is also true that a funding system that relies heavily on peer review, as do the UK research councils, will always choose proposals that make a case based on existing perceptions. Anything else tends not to be understood and is therefore potentially risky.

One of the advantages of the old block-grant system was that decisions to back a proposal were based on local knowledge.

Inevitably, some new ideas turn out to be rubbish but the odd one will be truly ground-breaking. I am doubtful whether the latter would survive the peer-review system, especially if the proposal came from a small, unfashionable university.

For many years I worked closely with a colleague who concentrated on natural products, isolating pure compounds from mainly tropical plants. He built a reputation based on skills in isolation and structure elucidation that were the equal of the best in the world.

As a result, he received lots of applications from students in developing countries who wished to learn how to do this kind of work. His lab was well equipped under the direct grant system and the only expenditure required from the student's country was for living expenses.

After the RAE was introduced it was decided that research should be funded on a basis of full economic costing. Rather than pay for the upkeep of the lab from a central source, all direct and indirect costs should be paid as part of project grants, awarded in a competitive process by the research councils and charities. This may have been part of the determination to crush the weaker institutions, since they find it difficult to compete for grants; I do not know.

The result was that many overseas students lost their opportunity to undertake research and eventually the lab closed. My former colleague emigrated to Australia; it was ironic that he took a reputation for top-class work with him.

He was sought after as a plenary lecturer at major conferences and had a stream of visitors from field ecologists, even Dian Fossey of 'Gorillas in the Mist' fame.

Very recently, the rules for the award of grants by the UK research councils have been changed. No longer is it a process that relies on the merit of the proposal alone; I am told that it is now necessary to be an established researcher with an outstanding record of attracting grants. There are starter grants for new academics but these do not go very far. Although it does not receive much publicity there has been an outcry in the scientific community at this attempt by the scientific establishment to annex even more of the available resource.

It is certain that my former colleague would not have been successful with the UK funding councils because the 'elite' universities are not involved in the general area of phytochemistry and there would be no big names supporting his work. It is now accepted that if you do not work in an area that has been approved by the elite you will stand little chance of a research career.

It is worth remembering that Albert Einstein was working in a patent office when he had his best ideas. Later, in a prestigious American university, with lots of time on his hands, he produced comparatively little.

In more recent times the technique of capillary electrophoresis, without which the human genome project could not have succeeded, was discovered in a technical institute in Finland. I doubt very much whether they would have received peer-reviewed funding in the UK.

How does all this relate to education? Those who are motivated to do scientific work will be restricted in the kind of work and the kind of place that can accommodate them. Smaller universities will not attract the best researchers and there will be less research carried out in many speculative fields that could yield big dividends. In general, it is the country as a whole that suffers from an academic class system.

'For whosoever hath, to him shall be given, and he shall have more abundance; but whosoever hath not, from him shall be taken away even that he hath'. Not good, is it?

Uniformity of thought

All social and academic establishments tend to promote shared attitudes, while pretending to embrace 'freedom'. Very often this leads to a decline in originality and performance, as the following anecdote shows.

For a time I had close contacts with a major British pharmaceutical company, which had made a breakthrough in the treatment of a chronic health condition. The company made a lot of money, which led to a change in recruitment policy. Before the big success they had gathered a group of chemists from different backgrounds, many without PhDs.

Some of their research seemed pretty aimless but one lab worker, without a PhD, started a line of work that many would have regarded as a dead end. When his compounds were tested they turned out to be the answer to a prayer, providing potent molecules with few side effects. The result was a blockbuster, that brought billions of pounds in profit.

As a result, the company could afford to employ the 'best' chemists available. They paid the highest wages in the industry and any vacancy would attract hundreds of applications. A substantial proportion had first class honours degrees from Oxford or Cambridge, a PhD or DPhil from the same place and post-doctoral experience with at least one well know chemist in the USA. At that time it was considered essential to have the qualification 'BTA' (Been to America) to be properly respected.

The result, in the long term, was that those responsible for innovation in the company all had similar backgrounds in synthetic organic chemistry and may have tended to think in the same way. The fortunes of the company declined, year on year. Common sense might suggest that a workforce looking above all for innovation and lateral thinking might benefit from staff with a variety of different kinds of experience.

At the time of writing the company has had to amalgamate with an overseas organisation and is struggling to survive. A similar pattern can be seen throughout 'Big Pharma'. GSK, for example, is an amalgamation of Glaxo, Allen and Hanbury's, Beecham's, Fison's and Smith-Kline-French. There is another reason for this, unconnected to uniformity of thinking, which is not directly relevant to my theme but is taken further in the next chapter.

Big Pharma

For some time I thought that this was too far removed from the main purpose of this book but there is some educational content here, more from the point of view of the UK economy than the individual.

At the time of writing Johnson and Johnson, in the USA, have been fined half a billion dollars for misleading patients about the side-effects of opioid analgesics. In recent years tens of thousands of people have died in the USA while using these drugs for pain relief and it is argued that the companies selling them had pretended that they were safe.

J&J are not the first pharmaceutical company to be fined a very large sum in the US courts; what follows is my attempt to explain why this happens. Corporate greed aka 'shareholder value' is one reason but there is a long history of confusing factors.

Going back to the 1930's, chemical research in drug companies was a matter of synthesising new molecules, a very difficult task compared to today, and testing them for any kind of activity that might be useful in medicine. There was no 'drug design'.

Chemists at May and Baker Ltd, in London in the 1930's, synthesised a range of compounds known as 'sulphonamides' which turned out to have antibacterial activity. There was no long-drawn-out process of clinical trial, the new compounds went straight to a few physicians who tested them on patients. Bear in mind that at this time there were no antibiotics and the available antibacterials were toxic. It is said that one of the series, sulphapyridine, was used to treat Winston Churchill in 1936. If he had died things might have turned out differently a few years later.

This approach to the discovery of new pharmaceuticals, and it was discovery rather than invention, continued until well after World War II. I remember meeting one chemist, in a large British pharmaceutical company, who was still just making compounds on a speculative basis in 1976.

From about 1960 there was a rapidly growing database of biochemical and pharmacological processes that began to make drug design possible. The structure of adrenaline had been known for some time and synthetic material was available for testing, showing that it had an effect on the heart and lungs as well as other organs. This led to the first beta-blocker, which reduced blood pressure and was a huge commercial success.

With enormous amounts of cash coming in, while the patent was valid, ICI Pharmaceuticals could pay huge dividends to shareholders. They could also invest in Alderley Park, employing hundreds more scientists in the search for more blockbusters.

Other companies, starting very modestly, had comparable success. Allen and Hanbury's in Hertfordshire were mainly known for blackcurrant pastilles but their chemists produced the first selective 'beta agonist' that relaxed the bronchi in asthma patients without drastic effects on the heart. Smith-Kline-French produced the first drug to reduce stomach acidity, which prevented stomach ulcers that would have required surgery. Fison's, Glaxo and Beecham's all produced useful medicines that had major effects on the companies' incomes. They all grew much larger. This was a time when the UK pharmaceutical industry was riding high; they became very popular with major investors.

In the 1970's I had a close collaboration with Wellcome Research Laboratories, who sadly no longer exist. They had a strong interest in muscle relaxants for use in surgery; most people know nothing about them but they save a lot of lives.

One of the Wellcome chemists had made a potential muscle relaxant that looked good in animal testing. He showed some data to a meeting of hospital anaesthetists on a Friday and one of them came to him afterwards. He said that he had nine patients coming in for bladder surgery on the following Monday: would it be possible to have some to try? This was in the 1960's, before the Committee on Safety of Medicines had been thought of.

The drug worked and all the patients survived but there were signs of an unwelcome effect on blood pressure, so the project was stopped. Very little money was wasted.

Partly as a result of the thalidomide disaster, pre-clinical safety testing of potential new medicines was greatly increased. In the following years, clinical trials became more and more extensive and very expensive in a futile attempt to guarantee safety. The companies had to attempt to protect themselves from litigation so every possible precaution had to be taken.

After this process had been rumbling along for a few years and ICI Pharmaceuticals had been separated as Zeneca, the company saw an opportunity to replace their successful beta-blocker with a more selective analogue; the original drug tended to cause asthma in susceptible patients and anyway the patent had expired.

A major effort saw them produce practolol, which had the required selectivity and was excellent in a number of clinical trials. To cut a long story short, when licensed and available to physicians in the USA, it caused a range of unpleasant side-effects in older people and had to be terminated. The clinical trials had all been conducted using healthy young volunteers.

In practice, there is no way to guarantee that a new drug will be safe in all patients under all circumstances but with Wellcome in the 60's there was next to no wasted effort, unlike practolol in the 70's.

With clinical trials now extending over several years, costs have ballooned into hundreds of millions, even a billion dollars. The sole reason is protection in the US courts against judgements intended to frighten even major companies. It is essential to be able to show that everything possible has been done to ensure safety.

An unanticipated outcome is that a new drug must have a large potential market to offset the cost of introduction. Antibiotics do not command a sufficiently large market, so there are virtually no new ones. It would not be possible for a company like May and Baker to bring sulphapyridine to the market in 2019; a modern-day Churchill would die if existing antibiotics did not work.

Government intervention will be required if we are to produce new drugs for small markets. Clinical trials will have to be kept much shorter and patients will have to accept a degree of risk. Specifically, drug companies will have to be given protection from litigation, at least where there is no other possibility of a financial return. The true risk can be tolerated, if there is no alternative treatment, by very close monitoring of the patient's condition, as used to be the case.

For much of the 20th Century the UK pharmaceutical industry was a major source of income. Share prices in the 'blue chip' companies were sky-high. The decline in the second half of the 20th Century closely matches the tendency for punitive damages in the USA. Without doubt, a few 'big pharma' companies have taken steps to protect their profits that overstepped the mark. They deserved to be punished but their actions are a sign of desperation. If you have spent hundreds of millions of dollars developing a drug it is very difficult not to take it to market.

Even where a drug goes through the whole process and is licensed for use in humans, small markets mean sky-high costs to the NHS; six-figure sums have been demanded for one year's treatment of a single patient to recoup costs and make a profit. Even worse, drugs have been synthesised and shown to be active in preliminary testing but further development could not be justified, even though patients were going to die. On one hand you have a patient suffering from a condition for which there is no treatment, on the other a laboratory with potential medicine but the two cannot be connected; the risk of litigation is too much to bear. The following scenario may help to illustrate the problem; the specific example is partly hypothetical but real examples occur all the time.

In an African village a young man sits in the dust outside his hut. He has sleeping sickness, caused by a parasite transmitted by biting flies. No treatment is available locally and even if he could afford to travel to a large city hospital, the only drugs available were developed in the 1920's and are very toxic, so the outcome of treatment would be uncertain.

In a university in the UK a group of scientists have been working on sleeping sickness, known scientifically as trypanosomiasis. They have been able to grow the parasites in the laboratory and have studied their biochemistry, which has led to the design of a potential drug which is very potent in the lab and expected to be non-toxic to humans.

There is no way that the patient can be treated with the drug without extensive clinical trials, which are incredibly expensive. Even if the patient could express a wish to try the medicine without clinical trial, the lawyers would have a field day, so the drug stays in the lab and the patient dies.

Ultimately the message is for the politicians: protect the pharmaceutical industry by permitting shared risk or watch it decline, with no new treatments for the majority of ailments.

Techniques

A lay person may get the impression that Nobel prizes are awarded for genius - this is often how they are represented in the media - but in most cases they are the result of expertise in a particular way of doing something.

My former colleague's expertise in identifying new chemical compounds from plants was in itself unremarkable, but without that expertise he would have been unable to help when asked to collaborate on a project to find out why leaf-eating monkeys are very choosy about the leaves they pick. His work was the first to establish a link between chemistry and ecology.

Going back much further in time, without the ability to make a telescope it would have been difficult to have studied the motion of the planets in our own solar system, let alone study other galaxies. Without microscopes we would know little about malaria and the parasite that causes it.

Always, the technique has to be developed first. Sometimes the next stage is quite mundane but application of the technique generates all the excitement: who was interested in X-rays until it was shown to be possible to get photographs of living people's bones?

It would be possible, with a little research, to come up with a long list of techniques that have enabled important advances, but rarely do we think of honouring the discoverers of the technique, such as capillary electrophoresis. In most cases the discoveries are incremental, with input from lots of observant, thoughtful people, but in the rare instance that the technique is rewarded it is usually just one or two figureheads who get the credit.

To improve the chances of new techniques being developed, we need to support the small players as well as the wealthy institutions. This is a potentially vital way for the UK to continue to be a world leader in research, although we need to be better at exploitation. For some reason we have been good at innovation but we can only continue in this vein if we back bright people wherever they happen to be. Even in a patent office or a technical college.

Grit

Young people in the UK have been described recently as 'the snowflake generation', meaning that they are mentally fragile. They are what use to be described as 'featherbedded'. Their parents and their schools bend over backwards to shield them from anything unpleasant.

One positive outcome is that they are far less inhibited than previous generations, relatively fluent when interviewed and able to sing in public in talent shows. In this they have become Americanised.

The down side is that they expect to be guided and protected all the time. Unfortunately, the world outside the home and the classroom is not so soft.

Some years ago, an eminent pharmacologist, a university professor, would say to anyone who would listen 'What we need is more bad lecturers.' This would be regarded as outrageous these days and with the requirement for 'bums on seats' totally unacceptable. His perception required explanation in the 1970's and even more so now.

In the days when poorly performing students were failed, their response to a poor lecturer had to be to take matters into their own hands, in other words to take responsibility for their own progress. If the subject was not presented clearly, they had to read around and discuss the topic with their friends, so that they could answer the exam question. In this way they learned more than being 'spoon fed'. It was a tough way to learn and required a degree of determination, or 'grit'.

Once accustomed to being mentally tougher, the students were more resilient and more capable of coping with a working environment. They had learned not just the subject matter but how to survive in a disordered world. For many, this was more important than the retention of facts, although they retained more factual knowledge as well. This is a conundrum for modern educational theory, which places all the emphasis on the competence of the teacher and the conduciveness of the environment in helping the young to learn. There is more to growing up than being docile.

When I assumed responsibility for a first year course, at the beginning of the student's first term at university, I had no delusions about the likelihood of any great attention to their studies. The first few weeks are a time for getting used to a new environment, making new friends and socialising. However, if socialising goes on too long, with no course assessments, it is possible to get into the habit of postponing work. The end of year exams come as a big shock and some very bright kids can fail or even drop out.

To avoid this, and to apply what I knew about consolidation of memory, I devised a routine. The course lasted for five weeks, with two sessions on my stuff each week. To begin, the students were given a concise summary of all the directly relevant information, just 33 A4 pages. I handed out a number of problems to solve and in the class sessions the students were told 'If you have done the work, put your hand up and one of us will check it. If it is correct you can go. If you haven't done it (most of them) get cracking and if you get stuck, put your hand up. Don't spend a long time trying to do it, if you are beginning to struggle put your hand up and someone will help'. There were no lectures.

On the Friday morning there was a multiple choice test. The students entered their answers on a specially printed sheet and when ready went to our brand new CAL laboratory and entered them on the screen. When they had all done it, the software marked the test and the results went straight onto the notice board, as percentages, where they had been told to look. The results were printed in mark order, with the student's names, and I drew a line at the faculty pass mark.

To begin with, there were lots of negative marks and about two thirds of the class failed. As expected, there was not a lot of work being done. The bottom mark was -26%. We had a high entry standard to the degree course so it was probably a new experience for the student who came bottom. What made an impact was not so much doing badly as seeing that some of the students had done relatively well. There is always a degree of competitiveness.

The format for the second week was the same but the results improved over all, with fewer fails and fewer negative scores. Without being nagged, they were getting the idea that the university required work as well as play. A few of the men still did not take work seriously, but after the third test they were in a small minority. By the final week, when the test covered the whole course, there were no fails.

In the following January there were departmental tests on all the first term material. In my module there was still an emphasis on understanding rather than facts but this was not a problem; they all did well. In the important exam in the summer, which would allow them to progress to the second year, they breezed through. I have never known such a confident group, they were assured that there would be no catch questions and they knew they could do problems that they had not seen before.

When I changed university I opted to teach the same course in the same way but I encountered two problems. First, there was to be no negative marking and second I was not allowed to put the student's names on the results sheet 'because they might be distressed'. In my opinion, it is far better to suffer a little embarrassment at an early stage than to fail at the end of the year.

Encouragement is always helpful but constructive criticism is essential, when appropriate. The alternative is that the student floats along, never facing reality, until somebody tells them. That is when they become really distressed. If the school or university does not oblige students to face reality, their eventual employer will, and it may not be wrapped in cotton wool.

Exam format

Many years ago, university exams in the subjects that I took tended to be based on essay answers. A normal exam paper in pharmacology would have eight questions, of which five had to be answered in three hours. The pass mark was normally 40%, so a passable mark averaged out at 8/20. In those days, first class honours were awarded for an average mark of 70% or more over several exams. Typically, an individual lecturer would only set and mark one question on any particular paper. For reasons that are not entirely obvious this tended to make 14/20 the mark for a very good answer. Five such marks would reach the standard for a first.

Unfortunately, relatively few students could reach the required standard on every answer and their aggregate mark would not reach 70%, so very few 'firsts' were awarded. In some departments it was possible to go several years without any. In my opinion this was too harsh. It was very noticeable that maths exams tended to produce the opposite, with marks varying from very low fails to very high passes, which caused problems when the university needed to keep students on course.

With many more students, the workload involved in marking essays grew considerably. It became routine for marking schemes to become mandatory, typically being a check list of things that should be mentioned in the student's answer, so that there was consistency of marking and a process that could be followed in the event of a student's appeal against the awarded mark.

Although marking schemes were introduced with the best intentions, one result was that style went by the board. Elegance of expression counted little against the phrase count, even though sometimes the student's answer gave little indication of clear thinking. To an extent, the baby had been thrown out with the bathwater. The marker's preference for clarity of expression was devalued in the search for objectivity.

In this environment, there is a lot to be said for multiple choice papers and computer marking. Personal preferences are removed entirely, as is the drudgery of marking a very large number of very similar papers.

With imagination it is possible to invent multiple choice questions that test a student's understanding, although not their ability to express themselves in English. My experience leads to the conclusion that many academics in science subjects find it difficult to think further than questions requiring recall, which strengthens the perception that all that is really required is memory.

This is not the place to give a catalogue of question formats that avoid the banal, but it is possible. In chemistry, for example, it is possible to provide a reaction scheme and ask whether it contains any errors. These might be, for example, an arrow pointing in the wrong direction, a wrong kind of arrow or a wrong sign of charge somewhere. With a little ingenuity there are various possibilities and, very importantly, the student does not need to have seen that exact reaction scheme before. It is entirely possible to separate those who understand from those who are just trying to learn the wallpaper patterns.

It takes much longer to set searching multiple choice questions compared to the average brain-dump regurgitation style but the marking takes no effort at all, a great blessing.

One feature in multiple choice question papers that I regard as essential is negative marking for incorrect choices. Suppose there are five choices: a correct answer scores +1, an incorrect answer -1/4. On this basis, random guessing tends to score zero, though luck plays its part. If there are only four choices, a wrong answer scores -1/3, and so on.

Without negative marking there is a high chance that an undeserving student will pass. If the pass mark is only 40%, as with the traditional essay-based paper, it is common to allow compensation down to, for example, 36%. With this rule, a student who has more marks in other exams can use the surplus to offset the shortfall, in which case the pass mark is actually 36%.

Now consider a multiple choice exam, which for simple arithmetic we shall assume to have 100 questions. If the student knows the answers to 20 questions and guesses on the other 80, he or she will, on average, score another 16 marks, making a total of 36%. With compensation this is a pass and the true pass mark is 20%, very handy if you have to keep bums on seats but not a good measure of ability.

If more poor students are passing, the same marking schemes will give much higher marks to the better performers, hence the recent suggestion that there are too many firsts and upper seconds. On some degree courses the 'good degrees' can constitute two thirds of the graduates. The reason for this is not because the students are working harder or that the teaching is better.

There is one perennial truth in the awarding of university degrees: if you give a degree to someone who does not deserve it, you have nothing to give those who do, because you have devalued the whole process. You can live in a fool's paradise for some time but eventually society will object, when employers continually find that some graduates are unemployable.

Computer Assisted Learning

The previous chapter touched on the use of computers in marking multiple choice exam papers and the beneficial effects this can have, if used with imagination. Elsewhere I have explored the benefits of repetition, which can be vital in providing a secure base for all kinds of learning. Computers are ideal for repetitious procedures, for obvious reasons. Practice in simple arithmetic is an example. There is a caveat, a warning against an excessive reliance on automated equipment, as follows.

One of the most important functions of a school is to get children accustomed to forming social relationships. People are individuals, often odd and unpredictable in their responses to new situations. We need to learn this from an early age but there is an increasing tendency for city children to be isolated until they go to school. They may be able to use software to find some form of entertainment but this does not require speech. Teaching software suffers from the same deficiency. People cannot be replaced by software, however sophisticated the programming that underlies the material.

Some people may not realise that a smart phone is a computer. There is a tendency for people, children included, to believe what they see on a screen. The effect is to give smart phones the power to spread misinformation, a form of malware that can be very dangerous.

Subject by subject

Religion

All the major religions start with rules directing our behaviour, preaching that we should be kind, forgiving and generous to those who are less fortunate. In every civilisation the state has adopted a religion for its own purposes, mainly to control the people with dire threats of the consequences of misbehaviour. This leads to a role in governance and the politicisation of the clergy. Once this happens, a life in the clergy starts to be attractive to those who seek power. The next step is to demonise other forms of religious belief, since the competing clergies see the others as rivals. A common outcome is religious war, about as far from the original concept of 'love thy neighbour' as you can get.

At the time of writing there are no major Protestant/Catholic confrontations but a religious war has resulted in misery for millions of followers of Islam in the Middle East. Everywhere, Shia and Sunni are killing each other, while innocent bystanders are forced to leave their homes, relying on the goodwill of others to survive. This is not what any prophet would have wanted.

In schools there is often a desire to 'bring children up' in a particular faith. For religious politicians the motivation is obvious since the youngsters will contribute to their future power base. For everybody else, allowing kids from different faiths to get to know each other at an early age has enormous advantages. Recent experience in Northern Ireland with mixed schools shows that the children perceive a basic truth, that there is no real difference between Protestants and Catholics. Of course, this threatens the power base of both faiths. Take religion out of the equation and there is no reason to hate one another and no bar to marriage outside the faith.

Some very rational people have tried to discredit all forms of religious belief, on the grounds that there is no objective evidence of a God. While this is true, there is no doubt that many people get enormous comfort from their faith. For some, religious belief keeps them going through difficult times. The alternative might be anti-depressants, which have some unwelcome side-effects.

It has become more common to ask a Humanist to speak at a funeral, rather than a representative of one of the religious faiths. For those who are convinced atheists, a non-religious ceremony is logical. However, Humanism does not offer support to the community on the same kind of basis as a vicar, for example, with regular contact and hopefully wise counsel.

The question we should ask comes down to a basic consideration of the role of religion in society: is it worth putting up with the bad aspects of religion to keep the good and how should schools deal with both? This is a difficult problem, given that in different communities there are strong historical and emotional allegiances. It is possible to make a few observations:

First, it is highly desirable to have mixed classes, which demolish the sectarian myths surrounding the 'others'.

Second, if all faiths have kind and loving belief systems, as many did originally, many of the differences disappear in mutual respect and affection.

Third, those who have no faith can still be brought up to be kind and loving and to respect those who do believe in God, or Gods.

Most of the problems can be traced to the religious politicians, who peddle hatred to shore up their own social position.

One problem that shows little sign of disappearing spontaneously is the insistence in some religions that Darwin's principle of natural selection is false. When his theory was first made public, Darwin was very anxious that the established church in England would object. He was justified in his concern but common sense prevailed after a few skirmishes with high level Anglican clerics. As far as I can determine, the position adopted by the Church of England is now that the text in the Christian bible is not always meant to be taken literally. I apologise if this is not the case.

To embrace 'creationism' as the only explanation of our existence requires that enormous quantities of information be set aside and rejected. The theory of evolution explains the existence of fossils, some closely related to modern man. With modern understanding of the role of DNA in shaping our form and our development, we have a well-researched basis for the mechanism by which one organism can change into another. With bacteria, which progress from one generation to another very quickly, evolution can be watched. It explains how bacteria become resistant to antibiotics, for example, in a process that closely mimics the development of different finches on separate islands in the Galapagos. Both are examples of natural selection.

Without accepting that human knowledge and understanding have come a long way since the Bible and the Koran were written, it is difficult for civilisation to progress. The stance taken by some clerics in Islam is very close to that taken by fundamentalist preachers in the Midwest of the USA. 'My mind is made up, do not confuse me with the facts'.

There is so much learned and understood about the origin of species that is useful, any social group that adamantly refuses to change its stance is obliged to live in the past. While some may welcome that, as a defence against change that they regard as dangerous, I doubt whether, in the long run, denial of something so clear and fundamental can be sustained. Personally, I wish that the atom bomb had never been invented, but we have to live with it.

From an educational point of view, we have to decide how to accommodate those who believe that the theory of evolution is wrong and who wish their children to believe the same. Either we separate the children into belief classes or we approach the subject from more than one viewpoint in mixed classes.

No doubt the religious politicians would prefer separation but in general this is a bad idea. If we wish people to get along in peace it is best that they become acquainted as children, otherwise all sorts of myths arise about 'them' and 'us'.

A basic question in tackling this problem is the attitude of the different religions to what most people regard as 'fact'. I can see no objection to showing children how bacteria become resistant to chemicals. It is possible to demonstrate this quite quickly and at minimum cost. I do not know how this can be explained if natural selection is denied but perhaps it can.

The general rule in science is that of 'Occam's razor'. William of Ockham, in the 14th Century, enunciated the principle that 'Given a choice of explanations, it is best to choose the simplest'. Natural selection explains so many things, it is difficult to look elsewhere.

Regarding human evolution, it is possible to show people fossils or pictures of fossils, as well as pictures of human footprints in solid rock, but the authenticity of these may be denied. Perhaps the way to approach this is to say to the class 'For those of you who believe the scientists, the explanation is ...'.

Some years ago, I assisted in the supervision of a PhD student who was asked to examine three species of plant, with a view to determining from their chemistry whether one was an evolutionary predecessor to the others. He worked on this for three years but when I asked him what his conclusions were he replied 'I believe in creation'. In the present era, he would have looked at the DNA of all three plants but little sense could have been made of the results without an acceptance of the principles of evolution. It is difficult to see how he could have progressed in his career as a scientist, but who knows? He clearly believed that God created all the compounds he had isolated.

In the long run, it is possible that common sense will prevail. If not, and bearing in mind that most of the world population has no knowledge of basic evolutionary theory, perhaps we shall subside into a state of ignorance and superstition, much like the Middle Ages. In my view, that would be a pity. Imagine, for example, if it was decided that the clerics in the Vatican were correct in their view that the Earth was the centre of the universe and that the sun went round the Earth. All the simplicity of the movement of the planets would be lost and all the calculations of how to send a spacecraft to Mars would not work. On reflection, perhaps the latter would not be so bad, it would save a lot of money.

Maybe the worst thing about creationism is that it encourages passivity: 'it is God's will'. A rejection of this attitude has underpinned all medical research and perhaps all research. Curiously, most of those who passively accept

God's will also accept the results of medical research, in the same way that vegans accept treatment with medicines that were investigated with the help of tests on animals. Is research of any kind automatically antireligious?

Science

Most people have an image of the scientist as someone who works in a laboratory, wears a white coat, and does mysterious things with complicated equipment. Sometimes this image is accurate but there are many scientists who work outdoors, wear ordinary clothes and sometimes use very little in the way of gadgets.

The unifying factor, with all scientists, should be the way they think. In every field of study, the 'scientific method' goes like this:

1) observe something that makes no sense

2) guess why it happens

3) make a prediction of what will happen if you change something specific, or look for something connected to the original observation that may have been missed.

If the outcome is consistent with your guess, you say that the guess has not been proved wrong. That does not mean that the guess is correct. So you

4) try to prove the guess wrong by a different test. And so on.

To make a simple analogy, consider 'noughts and crosses'. As a youngster, you may find that your older brother either draws or beats you every time. As long as your first move is random the same lack of success is guaranteed. If you decide to keep records of every game, you will discover that, when you go first, putting your cross in the centre square is better than putting it in the corner. If you put it into the middle square on an edge, you lose.

You could stop there, satisfied that you now tend to win as many games as your brother. If you can think like a scientist you will ask yourself whether there is a general principle and if so why? Using your imagination, you could try allocating a rating to each square, based on its influence in the game. The centre square is in the middle of four lines, vertical, horizontal and diagonal, so is very powerful. The corner squares are part of three lines and the middle squares of the edge rows are only part of two lines.

From this analysis, you might decide that you will put your 'X' or 'O' onto the highest ranking square available, with the proviso that you must block your opponents attempts to complete a row. On this basis you have a rule that works and you will never lose; much scientific progress is made using rules that work.

If this is as far as you go with noughts and crosses, you will have missed a significant feature of the game, an omission that will only become apparent if you move to more complex forms, specifically with a bigger grid and longer winning lines. At school I tried various formats but the best was a 13x13 grid, with the requirement to get five in a row to win. I call the game 'Quinox', for obvious reasons, and I can recommend it, I think it is better than draughts (chequers in the USA).

As a more important example of the scientific method, consider the progress of atomic theory. Until the early years of the 19th Century there was no concept of atoms or molecules, although the Greek philosopher Democritus had argued that constant chopping of matter into smaller and smaller pieces would eventually stop at pieces that could no longer be cut. He called the indivisible particles 'atomos'. When British chemists started to think about the basic structure of matter, John Dalton used observation and imagination to come up with his 'law of multiple proportions'. This was later clarified as molecular theory, in which the 'atomos', now called 'atoms', were the basic indivisible units that combined together in various ways.

At no point do you have 'faith' in your explanation, because faith implies total acceptance and experience teaches that new knowledge can always change the picture. About 100 years after John Dalton, it was shown that the indestructible atom could be blown apart, with the solid matter converted into an enormous amount of energy. The atom bomb was born and Democritus was proved wrong.

The first step in a scientific study has to be observation. Without reliable records there is nothing to hypothesise about (hypothesis being the upmarket word for 'guess'). We can see that Lord Rutherford's jibe about there being 'only physics and stamp collecting' was silly as well as offensive. Before you can start writing equations to describe the behaviour of things, someone has to collate information about the behaviour. All science starts from there.

We can see that the difference between science and other spheres of knowledge lies not in the collection of facts but in the way that those facts are viewed. Believe it or not, one of the most essential parts of the scientific method is imagination. At one time, the earth was thought to be the centre of the universe. Much later, after telescopes were invented, it was possible for Copernicus to *imagine* that the sun might be the centre, which explained a lot of strange observations regarding the way that the planets appeared to move.

From this description, it is possible to understand why an approach to teaching 'science' should not be based solely on recitation of established facts. To do so loses the spirit of this branch of philosophy. When reduced in this way, it is no different from the treatment of American history that James Loewen objected to. It is no wonder that imaginative children are turned off any discipline that seems to have no life, no vital spark.

Problem solving comes as close as we can get in a classroom to the scientific method. Please, teacher, provide some information and let the student work out what is going on! Remember 'William' (see under 'Memory versus Logic') the poor student who turned out to be the best in the class?

No doubt the traditionalists will argue that simply solving problems does not make an education; educated people carry information as well as skills. Of course this is true, you cannot solve problems without a basic set of familiar facts and techniques, but examining students solely on their recall does not identify those who might be capable of applying their knowledge to the unknown.

Reducing the arguments to practicality leads to a different approach to teaching. First, there has to be a base level of familiar, well understood principles, illustrated with examples. Then there has to be a process of involvement in areas that are designed to encourage invention and exploration. Always, part of the intention must be to identify and support those who can take the subject into a world which has not been described or has been described incorrectly. For those with little imagination there should be opportunities to fill a variety of niches in society that require systematic thought, to take other people's ideas forward and make sure that they are soundly based. Neither role requires an encyclopaedic memory for trivia.

None of this defines what a student needs to succeed in science. Imagination is very useful, as is a dogged determination when the going gets tough. To a large extent imagination has to be coupled to meticulous record keeping. I often had to remind research students that their lab book had to be a record of what actually happened. It is quite easy, when repeating an experiment, to write down beforehand what you expect to do. Then, if you are distracted and don't turn the heat off when you meant to, your record is inaccurate. It is not at all uncommon for repeats to give different results, even if you were sure you did the same thing each time. Of course, something was different.

In my case, during my PhD, one difference was the strength of the sulphuric acid. It came out of the same bottle but concentrated sulphuric acid absorbs water from the atmosphere when the bottle is opened. Tiny differences in concentration over a period of months made a big difference to the outcome.

Physics is a strange subject, requiring a good level of ability in maths as well as careful practical work. Even Albert Einstein had to get help with the maths when working on his theory of relativity. As a rule, physicists tend to say they 'understand' a series of observations when they have a mathematical equation that reproduces the results of experiments. Before opting for a career in physics the student needs to be content with a level of comprehension that is not the same as that in normal experience. Most people say that they 'understand' when they have a mental image that allows them to explain what happened. In normal life you can understand why your father became angry, if you have just hit a golf ball through his window. It is a nuisance, makes a mess and is an unnecessary cost to the household budget.

Physicists talk about the wave-particle duality of matter, meaning that extremely small 'solid' objects can behave as waves. You might be able to calculate the mass of a particle, but a wave? When we get to the atomic level we have to rely on maths to make predictions that can be tested, but whether this is really 'understanding' I am not sure.

Thinking back to Rutherford's dismissal of all subjects except physics as 'stamp collecting' I am reminded of my own experience with 'A' level zoology. Every question on the exam paper started with 'describe' or a variant such as 'list and describe'. In the 1960's biology was still in the gathering-of-data phase, from dead creatures. Ecology had not been invented. Studying live animals and the way they behave towards each other is much more interesting than dissecting the head of a dogfish.

Scientists

There is a strong tendency in many areas of science to place complete trust in maths. If we are not careful, this leads to a distrust of imagination and the ability of the scientist to use even common sense can disappear. This effect is most marked where maths is the backbone of the subject.

I am writing this during the coronavirus pandemic, in which a great reliance is being placed on mathematical modelling to guide government policy. Unfortunately the mathematicians were dissociated from the practice environment. If they had been aware of the details, they would have behaved differently and saved many lives.

At least two aspects were unknown to the analysts making predictions from the data. First, they were not aware that health workers moved between the care homes that housed the most vulnerable people, spreading the infection, and nobody thought to tell them, so their predictions of the rapidity of spread were underestimates. Second, the data provided by the NHS took time to collect and collate, so was always a week behind; again, nobody told them and they did not enquire.

In combination, the data analyses gave a false impression of the rate and severity of the epidemic, undermining the point of the whole endeavour. Thousands of lives were lost as a result, the consequence of poor communication, a lack of common sense and the division between those who gather and those who analyse.

While pure mathematics traditionally deals with the manipulation of numbers, applied maths is involved with the physical world. It is clear that, in the coronavirus pandemic, the scientists had lost sight of the need to be familiar with mere practical considerations. There should be a lesson here, for all disciplines to consider how the real world affects their work. The lesson for educationalists is that a premature retreat into the perfect world of mathematics should not be encouraged among school children. Maths is wonderful but the world is rarely 'pure'. Most importantly, all scientists need to retain the capacity for imagination, not just the subject leaders. Richard Feynman, the physics 'genius', was always exercising his imagination. He said that when he started as a student at MIT they had special sessions to encourage thought processes that were not merely following the maths. I don't know if any UK science department has ever done that.

There is a strong tendency in schools for children to be encouraged to specialise in the subjects in which they get the highest exam marks. The down side to this is that budding mathematicians drop all the 'humanities' very early and do not learn much biology, which covers a huge variety of quite different topics and specialisations. The encouragement to concentrate on numbers can easily lead to teenagers and then adults giving up all familiarity with the real world, when their innate tendencies already lead them in that direction.

The education they need, to be healthy, social animals, is the exact opposite. We should aim for mathematicians who are comfortable as human beings, not shy nerds who cut themselves off. They might be more inclined to take more interest in the data they analyse, as well as living happier lives.

Incidentally, over-specialisation at an early age applies to the humanities as well. No child should be encouraged to say 'I can't do maths', when all they really need is an education that goes more slowly and takes more interest in them as individuals.

Practical classes

Volumetric analysis has always been part of a chemistry course, usually in the first year at university. It was also 'covered' on A Level courses. For those who have never had the pleasure, the idea, in its simplest form, is to place a measured amount of substance A into a flask and introduce measured amounts of substance B, usually from a graduated tube called a burette, until the exact quantity of B has been added to react precisely with the measured amount of A. There are some niceties that do not matter for now but the object is to measure either A or B. If we know the exact strength of A we can find the strength of B and vice versa.

It is really very simple but the challenge comes in being accurate enough to get a precise answer. As a result, almost every student wants to compare his or her result with those on either side. Those with few scruples and no confidence will compare their result and very often adjust their figure to agree with the majority. Since the only purpose of the exercise is to develop an accurate technique, cheating is not acceptable, but they nearly all do it. One effect of trying to be careful, while lacking expertise, is that an exercise that should take ten to twenty minutes would occupy the whole three-hour timetable slot.

To stop the student's cheating I tried a variation that worked beautifully but to explain what I did I have to use a few chemical terms. The syllabus task was to titrate a solid, benzoic acid, with sodium hydroxide solution from the burette. The strength of the sodium hydroxide was known very accurately. They all did it and the correct answer was that the benzoic acid was 100% pure, to a precision of +/- half a percent. To be pedantic, the correct conclusion should have been that the sample contained the *equivalent* of 100% benzoic acid, since no tests had been made to be certain that it was as labelled. Lots of students got it right but many who didn't fiddled their result.

I decided to set a test, which was not pass/fail but with plenty of time for repetition if a student got the wrong answer. The difference was that the solid being analysed was not necessarily benzoic acid but a similar compound that looked similar and reacted in the same way. I had a range of these and we also made up several sodium hydroxide solutions of different strengths. The students were led to believe that their sample was benzoic acid but they were labelled A, B, C and so on; we kept accurate records of who got what.

The effect was that the correct answer could be anything from about 70% purity to maybe 120%, each accurate answer being precisely known to us. If they got it right they were told that the course was finished. If wrong they had to come back the next week and do it again. Several students went into their sixth week before the penny dropped, but one of them, who had a very accurate titration, fiddled his result to be 100% and had to do it yet again.

This long-drawn-out process showed me several things. First, as we would all expect, that honesty is important. Second, that lack of confidence is a major factor in breeding dishonesty. The most important lesson is that the normal way of running the class, as a series of exercises, was largely futile. It did not teach technique and it confirmed the students' belief that cheating was worthwhile.

While this specific remedy is limited in scope, it suggests that many practical classes, in different areas of science and technology, could be approached with a bit more imagination.

Often the stumbling block is one of technique. I could ask you to compare samples using infra-red spectroscopy but only if you know how to use the equipment; very often the whole purpose is to teach the technique. Rather than simply give a list of instructions and ask the student to follow a recipe, as is normal, it would be more interesting to divide the task into two. The first part, that we might call familiarisation, would be closely specified. We might provide instructions on how to obtain a spectrum from a liquid and then from a solid since the two techniques are very different.

In the second part we might ask if three samples are all the same, using their infra-red spectra. No two students, or pairs of students, would be given the same compounds to compare.

A comparable approach was used in the pharmacology classes I encountered in my final year as an undergraduate, except that we were asked to use animal tissues in thermostatted, oxygenated baths of Ringer solution instead of a spectrophotometer. Those classes were very challenging.

I am insufficiently familiar with other science subjects to devise comparable scenarios for teaching and assessing practical techniques but I would be surprised if it is not possible. The intention, as always, should be to challenge and stimulate rather than simply ask the student to follow a list of instructions. We should also remember that repetition leads to familiarity, retention and confidence.

Ecology

Of all the subdivisions of science, the one that has the greatest significance for survival is ecology. For that reason it is worth special attention in schools and a place here, separate from the general discussion of 'science'.

Everything that we do to the natural environment has unexpected consequences. It has recently been observed that microfibres, from washing the synthetic material used to make a 'fleece', pass into the water that goes down the drain and through the water treatment works. They are not biodegradable and end up in the sea, along with the microspheres that are used in cosmetics. These tiny pieces of plastic are then taken in by living creatures and may be fatal. If not, the primary organism becomes food for the next stage in the cycle, tiny fish which grow and are eventually eaten by us. The long-term effect of these tiny pieces of plastic, inside us, we do not yet understand.

When a farmer grows a crop on a large scale, the organisms that feed on the crop have a literal field day. As they multiply they find plenty of food, to the point where they have a drastic effect on the crop yield. The natural recourse is to pesticides, typically insecticides: nicotine is a potent insecticide and it was inevitable that scientists would try to find variations on the molecular structure. They were very successful, giving rise to the 'neonicotinoids'.

Unfortunately the neonicotinoids are too good. They penetrate all parts of the plant, even the pollen, which is eaten by bees. In small quantities the dose is not fatal, but it gets into the brains of the bees, with the result that they fail to find food and die from starvation. Without bees a wide range of crops will not be pollinated, so yields will decline. The affected crops are all the fruits, from apples to raspberries, and for example oilseed rape; almost any crop that produces seeds from nectar-bearing flowers relies on insects.

There has been a huge decline in insect populations in Europe in recent years, as insecticides have become more effective. Most people do not have a high regard for creepy-crawlies, apart from butterflies, but without them we may be in deep trouble; the effects are yet to be seen.

Ecosystems are complex and unpredictable, as was shown in Yellowstone National Park in the USA when wolves were re-introduced, in the face of extreme opposition from local people.

It should be acknowledged that wolves are present on all continents, including Europe, as they have been since before humans arrived. Although the numbers are small, they are part of the ecosystem in, for example, Spain, France and Italy. In Eastern Europe they are numerous but do not constitute a threat to people, although livestock may be taken if not protected.

In Yellowstone they were re-introduced because they are a natural part of the ecosystem, the top predator. The effect was remarkable and largely unpredicted. Without the top predator, deer numbers had risen excessively, with damaging effects on their preferred areas: tree seedlings were eaten off at ground level and soil erosion meant that streams ran muddy.

The effect of the wolves was to reduce the deer population, as expected, but also to move them around. The favourite places for the deer became the favourite places for the wolves, so the deer moved on. The areas they left immediately started to regrow young trees, including the species that beavers like. The beavers built dams, which slowed the water down and dropped out the silt.

The streams ran clear, which benefitted the fish that needed clean water to spawn. And so on; a very wide range of creatures gained from the presence of wolves.

Most people live in cities and very few have any contact with healthy ecosystems, although human welfare depends on the natural world. If the subject is not given priority in education we may find that city politicians will not help to protect their heritage, through ignorance. Many city dwellers have no idea where their food comes from.

Modern languages

I have no doubt that learning other people's languages is beneficial; we need to be able to talk to each other. My problem with the way that French and German were taught to me concerns the overly academic way that the subjects were approached. Great emphasis was placed on grammar, which is nice but not essential; even native French and German speakers get the grammar wrong quite often. More importantly for me, I believe from what I have read that children learn their parent's language in a different way. Not just by repetition but using a different part of the brain compared to those who approach the task academically.

I know that most of the German that I remember now came from two periods of four weeks living in Germany with two families, none of whom spoke any English. The stuff I learned in passing 'O' level has almost entirely disappeared.

As far as French is concerned, I found that spending a month working in France was far more useful than 'Mettez la forme correcte du verb'. Watching French television in the evenings, I found simple quiz shows like 'Fa si la' and 'Questions pour un champion' to be useful because they tended to repeat the same simple phrases.

While international student exchanges are unlikely to occur on a large scale, satellite TV could offer some interesting possibilities, since it is now possible to re-orientate the dish to receive a wide range of national broadcasting stations.

Personally I have found Bavarian TV somewhat limited in scope. Most programmes, at least in the afternoon, seem to be confined to cookery demonstrations or religious ceremonies, but it is still possible to learn like children do.

Music

I have to say that music, in my grammar school, was very badly taught. This was not the teacher's fault, the school was academic through and through, so music was taught in the same way. We learned about crotchets, minims and semibreves, about bass clefs and treble clefs, but not much else. It was only later, when music as a curriculum subject was dropped, that I started to learn to play the clarinet, by practice and imitation. I owed this entirely to a friend who had discovered traditional jazz, very popular in Britain at that time. His favourite, then and I think now, was Chris Barber's band, while I preferred Acker Bilk. I still think Acker was the finest clarinettist in the genre, although I never liked 'Stranger on the shore'.

For me, the joy of music was not the academic structure but melody, harmony and rhythm. Most so-called classical music lacked rhythm, while 'modern jazz' often lacked melody and harmony.

In my early teens, skiffle became very popular. I can still remember two boys playing guitars, another boy on tea-chest bass and a fourth on washboard, playing together in a classroom one lunchtime. I thought it was wonderful. The chords were simple and the tunes equally so, but they made music.

If music is to be popular in schools it needs to be participatory. There is huge enjoyment to be had from making music together, whether singing or playing instruments. I think most of my school enjoyed the end of year carol service because we could sing together. Much more could have been done to involve the pupils in performing music.

Continuing the theme that runs through this book, trying to teach music from a basis of academic theory is a dead loss for most children (the approach may have changed from my day). It sucks the life out of something that ends up being very important for a large proportion of the population. Although music becomes a part of many people's lives, it is as consumers; 'pop-pickers' as the disc jockey Alan Freeman used to say. Schools can do so much more to encourage children to make music themselves.

The bottom line is, as always, to keep it simple. Teach a girl or boy how to hold an instrument, how to tune it and how to get basic sounds from it, a relatively short learning curve. Teach them a few chords, on a keyboard or guitar, or a few simple tunes on a melody instrument, and they can play together. The rest is magic.

Once the initial phase is over, and those who do not enjoy it have given up, may be the time to explore different instruments. There is a world of difference in the skills required to play a clarinet compared to a piano: the latter requires the hands to do different things at the same time, while the clarinet requires both hands but in sequence. And there is percussion, which even the tone deaf may take to.

Getting sounds out of a brass instrument such as a trumpet is a challenge. This is not a good starting point, kids respond to encouraging feedback. Neither is a violin, because the absence of 'frets' leads to a wide range of horrible sounds. It can take a long time to learn to place the fingers on exactly the right places on a violin or cello, with a probability that the learner will give up. To a certain extent, the trombone has problems common to both the trumpet and violin, although bum notes played on a trombone are far less offensive than on a violin.

To summarise:

pick the right instruments. Please avoid the recorder, their pitch is always sharp and they do not combine well with other instruments. So-called penny whistles are much better and a lot cheaper.

give the kids time to come to terms with simple concepts, not confused by terminology

allow time for experiment

once past the initial phase, let them play together

encourage the development of a sense of rhythm, particularly when playing together

do not try to 'sell' orchestral music, even if your favourite composer is Mozart, this may come later but may not.

do not express disdain for popular music, let them bang, hoot and twang to their heart's content.

Inevitably some of the children will make faster progress than others. They may have a natural aptitude or a more supportive home. Whatever the cause, let them play together if they wish, in whatever groups they wish.

What has all this to do with survival? I shall come to that later.

Art

By this I mean drawing and painting, a fairly narrow definition but the one that was used in all schools at one time.

Very few homes have the equipment to allow children to develop their drawing skills. Equally, very few parents have those skills or the knowledge to teach them. While practice is fundamental, there are techniques that can be developed to improve artistic ability.

To appeal to children, it is necessary to use materials that can make a statement. Wishy-washy water colours are not what children respond to. Basic technicalities such as the pen, pencil or brush, need to be attended to by the teacher. A hard pencil is useless.

Some active teaching is required, along the lines of, for example, 'This is how to draw a face' 'This is how to control perspective' and so on. These aspects are perhaps less obvious and benefit from early help. Most kids can learn to play a simple tune on a penny whistle but very few could paint a face without help.

As with music, the survival angle comes later.

Management

After World War 2 there were a large number of car manufacturers in the UK; off hand I can remember Triumph, Rover, Morris, Austin, MG, Landrover, Singer, Hillman, Ford, Vauxhall, Sunbeam, Humber, Riley, Aston-Martin, Rolls-Royce, Bentley and Standard. There were very few foreign cars sold in Britain. In the 1960's competition from German, French and Japanese cars began to eat into the market, with the result that there were amalgamations and bankruptcies. Triumph, Rover, Austin, Morris and MG became the British Motor Company and then British Leyland. Jobs, variety and skills were lost but even centralisation, with its economies of scale, failed to save them.

Rover always had a reputation for high build quality but as part of British Leyland the bodywork got thinner and rust became a major issue, even within three years of manufacture. In contrast, BMW in Bavaria stuck with high build quality through difficult times and eventually emerged as the company that it is today, selling huge numbers of profitably expensive cars all over the world.

One reason for the eventual demise of British Leyland was labour relations. The work force acquired a reputation for awkwardness and greed, led by 'Red Robbo'. The conclusion was that UK workers were workshy and one by one car plants across the UK closed down. The exceptions were Vauxhall and Ford (both companies American-owned) and the specialist manufacturers such as Landrover, Aston-Martin, Rolls-Royce and Bentley.

Some years later, the major Japanese manufacturers Honda, Nissan and Toyota opened factories in England. Peugeot bought an existing car plant in Coventry. Suddenly, British workers became the best in the world; hard-working, careful and productive. What made the difference?

One possibility is that, in the Honda factory in Swindon, the boss wore the same clothes as the rest of the workforce and ate in the same canteen. There were also suggestion boxes, for employees to contribute their ideas for improved productivity. Many of these ideas were acted on. The general principle was that all the workers were respected and felt part of a communal effort. It is sad that, at the time of writing, the Honda plant is to close, with the loss of 3,500 jobs. The reasons given have nothing to do with the workforce.

Peugeot eventually closed their plant in Coventry but praised the quality of the workforce as the best they had. It was simply that their market share had gone down and as a French company they had to conserve French jobs. The lesson from Honda and Peugeot is that ownership matters; selling out to foreign investors leads to insecurity.

In 1966 I got a temporary job in a paint factory in Bristol. The working conditions were dangerous and unhealthy, which did not help, but a detail that impressed me at the time was the canteens: there were four! I ate in the manual workers canteen, the lab staff had their own place, the managerial staff ate separately and the directors, of course, had a privileged environment. It was the class system gone mad.

'Management' courses have become more popular in recent years, perhaps because some British companies recognised that their management practices were very poor compared to those overseas. Unfortunately, it is not possible to take an 18-year-old, send him or her to college for three years and expect that the work force will respond positively to someone who is not familiar with them as people or with the work that they do. It is a reinforcement of the class system to bring in someone in a 'superior' position and expect the shop floor to respond.

Company directors tend to have psychopathic personality traits more commonly than the population as a whole. This leads to treatment of people as a commodity, along with premises and feedstock; a cost to be controlled by whatever means is available. This is the extreme version of 'them and us' that led to the demise of British Leyland. Treat the employees without consideration and they will respond in a similar manner. Harsh working conditions may result in financial success for a time, but only if there is a queue of unemployed people, on the verge of starvation.

Most employees will show loyalty to the organisation they work for if they are treated with respect. Although the profits may not be shared equally, a structure that gives everybody a say in what goes on will work better than any other. In the UK, the John Lewis stores employ people as 'partners', with the result that they all expect good performance from their equals. A shop assistant who is not attentive to a customer's needs will be answerable to those around them, not just management.

There is a range of intelligence and wisdom in all areas of society. Stratifying the population into upper, middle and lower classes helps nobody. Specifically, because somebody has the energy to start a company and see it through the early years does not mean that he or she will be humane, or wise or have sufficient 'people skills' to make a success in the long term. Equally, an organisation that succeeds over many years through enlightened treatment of its employees may be taken over and fail if the new owners have bone-headed psychopathic tendencies.

The bottom line is simple: good managers are either born or they develop empathy in their formative years. Management at its most effective involves people working with people, understanding each other's problems and adapting to changing circumstances with good will. Relationships come from the heart, not from lecture courses.

Why do British companies refuse to have workers on the board? Even Conservative governments have considered making this compulsory. A German friend recently explained to me that, with obligatory worker representation on the company board, workers generally are much less likely to go on strike. As he said 'They are not inclined to saw off the branch they are sitting on.'

At the time of writing British Airways pilots have gone on strike, despite the offer of a substantial pay rise. They are striking because they see a better way to run the company, with a profit sharing scheme that would include all employees, not just the pilots. The management have refused even to discuss the idea, despite its success in companies like John Lewis. The pilots' suggestion of shared returns is certain to be beneficial: who would go on strike if the result was a loss of profit?

Economics

This might seem to be a strange suggestion for inclusion in a school syllabus but the way that finances work and the frequent mistakes made in all parts of society suggest otherwise.

To start I shall introduce the concept of 'entropy' and suggest a parallel with the way that government and businesses work.

In the early 19th Century, engineers were experimenting with ways that heat could be converted into motion. When wood or coal are burned heat is produced, but it was observed that a ton of wood produced less heat than a ton of coal, so coal had a potential heat content greater than that of wood. Clearly, if you wanted to get a train from Stockton to Darlington it would be best to use coal rather than wood, since it occupied less space for the same return.

At some point in the development of steam engines it was found that coal varied according to where it was mined. Some coal burned more slowly, although the total amount of heat produced might be the same; it just took longer.

This was important when pulling a train, since slow burning coal would make the train run too slowly. At the time this was a mystery and the early investigators gave it the name 'entropy'. The available heat they called 'enthalpy', defining two aspects that they needed to quantify. This led to the concept of 'thermodynamics' as the study of the conversion of heat into movement.

How does this relate to economics? Let us suppose that a builder acquires land and gets planning permission for two houses. He borrows money to buy materials and pay the workforce and calculates the selling price. He recruits all the people required for the project and arranges for them to be available at the right time: he doesn't want the electrician to arrive before the walls and roof are complete.

To begin with all goes well. The weather is good, the foundations are laid and the first house is built. Cash flow requires that the first house needs to be sold before the second house is started, and it is.

Arrangements are made with the bricklayers, joiners, plumbers and electricians to come back at the right time. Then the rain starts, the brick lorry gets stuck on the access road and there is a delay. The bricklayers are paid piecework rates and they have no bricks, so they go elsewhere, with a promise to come back. The lorry is pulled out of the mud, at some expense, and the bricks are unloaded, but the bricklayers are busy, because the rain has also delayed the other job they are working on. The further delay means that the joiners find other work.

All the time there are delays means that there is no cash flow to pay for the loan, which has to be renegotiated at extra cost. It is close to a disaster, as winter closes in and the rain continues, the temperature drops and it is too cold to lay bricks.

If the analogy is not apparent, let me clarify the issues. In both cases the difference between success and failure is the rate at which events unfold. If the train goes too slowly or the house is not built in time, the outcome is not good.

With the steam engine, the return from burning coal is measurable in the first place as heat, then motion and finally delivery of passengers to their destination, with a cash return. With the house the return is first the building, then a place for someone to live and finally a cash return to the builder and his employees.

In both cases, the entropy factor is directly connected to the likelihood of something going wrong. In effect, it is a measure of the probability of a cock-up. The more variables there are in the process the greater the chance that some random factor will interfere. This is common sense, enshrined in the everyday experience of all those who do practical work:

'The best laid schemes of mice and men gang aft agley'

Murphy's law: 'if something can go wrong, it will' (this is also known as sod's law).

As far as I know, this has not been referred to as entropy before, but reduction of entropy has been a key factor in business success for many years. Fairly recently, Amazon has become the most successful retailer on the planet by reducing entropy to a minimum. One-click shopping has it all. If you are selling something on the high street, you are relying on a series of events going in your favour.

Suppose that Mrs Smith needs a new washing machine. She can go to a retail outlet but first has to choose where she goes; the local shop or the mall. If she is unwell she may postpone the trip or stay closer to home. In the mall there may be several retailers selling washing machines. Perhaps her neighbour is going to a large town where there are different choices and offers her a lift. All these 'what-ifs' add up to greater uncertainty.

In contrast, consider the problems that the UK government has had in introducing 'Universal Benefit'. Most analysts and most politicians, from right and left, believe that it is a good idea. Essentially, the system will be simpler and cheaper to administer; the savings can be costed. The analogy with thermodynamics is that the cash return equates to the 'enthalpy'.

In practice, delays in paying the benefit caused hardship to large numbers of people. Some very poor people could not pay their rent and lost their homes, with drastic consequences, even where the delay was only a month or two. The government was not saving money by the delay, it was just a cock-up.

This is why nobody in politics should be allowed to influence policy or processes who does not have practical experience of the unpredictability or 'entropy' of everyday, normal life. Equally, taking advice from academics is not a good idea if you have no means of judging that advice. As a rule, the academics can calculate the cost of a policy in terms of the cash equivalent or 'enthalpy' but gauging the 'entropy' is much more difficult. The uncertainty factor causes delays and delays cost money. If you need an example, think of the Edinburgh tram project. It might have been anticipated that laying track in an old city might have complexities but the costing was established as if Edinburgh was still a green field. The delays and cost overrun were enormous. Many predict that HS2 will probably be the same. If they are correct, this is managerial failure on a grand scale.

One of the consequences of ill-prepared politicians taking huge responsibility without knowledge, experience or wisdom is that they fall back on dogma. In the Conservative ranks, the commonest dogma is that 'private is good, public is bad'. This has led to the privatisation of the public utilities, gas, water and electricity. For the politicians there were two positives; a short term boost to the 'public purse' and the avoidance of unpopular rises in charges when under public ownership. After privatisation the new owners put prices up to pay their shareholders, but the unpopularity is directed at the company boards.

More recently, it was decided to privatise the probation service, even though it was working quite well. The result has been an unmitigated disaster, with a loss of £450 million and much larger numbers of prisoners re-offending.

If the connection with my general theme is not obvious, it is twofold. First, education is far more than learning from books, however well written the books are, and second we need a means of selecting our representatives that is not left in the hands of the 'establishment'. Perhaps would-be politicians should be subjected to a series of tests, with published results. The tests would have to be carefully structured to find the people who could think clearly and anticipate real-world problems, not just remember loads of facts. I don't for a moment think this will ever happen.

One final point. Economics has been called 'the dismal science' but it is not a science at all. In physics, we can measure the effect of temperature on a gas in a box and find that the pressure goes up in line with the temperature. Alternatively, we could use an expandable container and find that the pressure stays constant but the volume increases as the temperature goes up. We can make the measurements over and over again, wherever we like; the result is the same. In economics we can make observations one day and find that the next day is different, depending on the mood of the investors. Computers can be used to make investment decisions but they cannot be programmed to predict how human beings will behave.

Personal finances

It is very difficult to control expenditure if you are not numerate. In my youth, the wages of manual workers were paid in pound notes and coins at the end of the week; relatively few people had a bank account. Money was real and tangible; if you spent it you could relate to the reduction in cash in your pocket and many people were careful to make sure that they did not run out. If you spent it in the pub or the betting shop before you had bought the week's groceries you would go hungry.

The result was a kind of reinforced numeracy, to back up what you had recited and practised at school. The majority of people react to reality more than theory.

Since the invention of the credit card, bank profits have gone through the roof and the act of spending money has become divorced from reality. You can wave the plastic at a gadget in the shop and there is no pain. At the end of the month the bank will charge a hefty rate of interest on what you owe, unless you pay it off immediately. I would guess that the driving force for the introduction of credit cards was not shopper's convenience but bank profit.

Credit card charges are always expressed as the Annual Percentage Rate, or APR. Some years ago I started some correspondence in 'Chemistry in Britain' by pointing out that many undergraduates had no idea what 'percentage' meant. This was in a chemistry context, relating to the concentration of chemicals in a solution. I was assailed from all quarters by school teachers who claimed that the idea of 'percentage' was out of date. They used the concept of 'molarity' instead. Without going into technicalities, 'molarity' requires you to know the precise structure of the substance being dissolved.

In the world generally, there are many examples where you do not know the chemical structure, or you may be dealing with a mixture. If you are diluting treacle with water, for example, the best way to be accurate may be to say 'make a 10% solution'.

The undergraduates who were struggling with 'percentages' were academically among the top few percent in the country. What chance do the rest have with 'APR'? Sadly, poor people with no bank account may suffer worst, because the interest rates charged by money lenders are extortionate.

If we are to avoid the situation where tens of thousands of people get into financial difficulty every year, we need to make sure that they can handle some simple concepts, and the first of these is 'percentage'. Like most subjects that we should teach at school, the requirement is for repetition, reinforcement and revisiting. It will have no impact with most kids if it is covered in one or two lessons and never picked up again. Every opportunity should be taken to make sure that the class still understands, every year. This is truly education for survival.

I would guess that one way of getting the reality of personal finance across to children would be to carry out transactions with real money, taking it away when the interest is due.

Advertising

In recent years, two activities that have embraced advertising are money lending and gambling. Both require a level of numeracy if the 'consumer' is not to become a victim.

More widely, the consumer needs to be streetwise if he or she wishes to avoid wasting money. The truth is simple: most advertising involves a level of misrepresentation, to persuade you to buy something that you do not really want.

Although there are laws to protect the consumer from the worst excesses of the advertising industry, much of what goes on treads a fine line. A typical example is the companies that offer guidance in choosing home or car insurance. In most cases they will give you a comparison between a range of providers but the range may not include the best deal; they will offer you only the insurance companies that pay them to be on the list.

In recent years advertising has spread from newspapers, magazines and TV to various internet sources. The advantage to the seller is that the internet providers can analyse your browsing habits to target the adverts. Have a look on line for a new washing machine and for some time afterwards you will get pop-up boxes offering you different makes.

The most curious aspect of internet advertising is the enormous value that investors perceive in this new industry. Google, Facebook, Snapchat and so on have made multibillionaires out of their founders, for doing very little, although of these Google has provided a very useful search tool. Curiously, it is not the search engine itself that has brought the profits.

None of the advertising vehicles publicise the basic reality, that the profits come from you. When ITV started in the UK, consumers were pleased that there was no charge for the service, unlike the BBC. They were not told that everything they bought, after screen advertising, was more expensive. It had to be, to pay for the adverts. There is no such thing as a free lunch. The annoying aspect is that everybody pays for more expensive goods, not just those who watch ITV or browse the internet.

In my opinion, it would be appropriate to teach schoolchildren how to be discerning in their response to adverts. It would be fun for the kids, too. We have all seen adverts for cosmetics which say in small print something like '75% of 57 women agreed that this product gave them the appearance of having fewer wrinkles'. The impression is created that a major share of lots of women are endorsing the product.

Imagine that you were one of the testers and that you had been given a pot of cream to smear on your face every day for two weeks. At the end of the test period you would be visited by a pleasant woman who would ask you very nicely 'Do you think you have fewer wrinkles now than before the test?'. Most people like to be friendly and polite to someone who speaks to them very nicely; most of us have learned not to be rude, so we agree. The fact that 25% did not agree says a lot.

If you were part of a clinical trial of a new medicine, the trial would be strictly organised to avoid bias. This usually means a 'double-blind crossover', in which there would be a comparison of the hoped-for active medicine with a placebo, with neither the doctor or patient knowing which was which. The face-cream tests are charades, to give spurious credibility.

'Buyer beware' would not be a bad title for a school module. It would have a better chance of acceptance than double maths.

The misrepresentation in adverts is a relatively trivial example of something that politicians have taken to calling 'fake news'. The public have always been misinformed on a selective basis, sometimes with the best intentions. At the beginning of World War II the news was often so bad that it was not made public. More recently, politicians of all kinds have been complaining about fake news, which may be justified or may be a way of covering up the truth. Who is to judge what is fake? Ultimately, the public end up not trusting anything that they are told.

Probably the best we can do is to teach our children to be sceptical, starting with advertisements.

Politics

The first question you might ask is 'Do we really need to teach our kids about politics?' Some universities do and presumably they manage to keep a balance between opposing views by presenting both. The arguments are inevitably presented to a small number of students; the rest of the population must form their own thoughts or, perhaps more commonly, take no interest whatsoever. Taking no interest seems like a good way to undermine democracy.

Normally a political discussion tends to polarise into right and left wings but since a lot of people have mixed views, some right some left, the division is arbitrary. In discussing politics, however, it is convenient to examine both sides, even though most economies are mixed.

Thinking first of capitalism, we can find some positive aspects. From the consumer's point of view the most beneficial is competition between suppliers, generally a feature of free markets. Taking cars and 'white goods' as examples, the price of both is kept down and the quality improves because the manufacturers and sellers are competing. This need not be confined to capitalist systems but tends to be.

Another, perhaps the most characteristic feature of capitalism, is an eagerness to exploit opportunities and the relative lack of barriers to this. This turns out to be a two-edged sword, because exploitation can be at the expense of people and of the natural environment. Think of oil palms in south-east Asia, where huge tracts of rain forest have been cleared at the expense of local people and animals like the orangutan. Some profit-making enterprises have had drastic effects on the world climate and continue to do so because they pretend otherwise. It is reminiscent of the tobacco companies, who continued to advertise their wares and attract new smokers even in the absolute certainty that they were causing lung cancer and a variety of other diseases.

On the other hand, capitalist enterprises have found cures for many ailments, far in excess of those discovered elsewhere. Whichever way you look at it, capitalism does tend to be linked to wealth creation, creating a surplus that can lead to further inventions. In the search for new medicines, there is an unexpected problem. When a company makes a breakthrough and enormous profits follow, it tends to re-invest in increasing the workforce to make further discoveries. Unfortunately, history shows that the chance of finding more than one blockbuster is small, which means that the company struggles and may have to fold or amalgamate.

More importantly, projects that require major investment, without guaranteed returns, tend to be unattractive to those who regard money as the most important element in existence. Attempts to make medicines safer have backfired, with 'ambulance chasers' in the USA attempting to subvert the whole process of drug discovery to their own greedy ends. The result is that no capitalist pharmaceutical company can spend money on the development of antibiotics, for example, because there is not enough profit to be made.

The weaknesses of capitalism are innate and have to be controlled by legislation. Without control, the inevitable tendency is that successful companies either conquer others or simply buy them out, with a rapid trend towards monopoly.

The second problem with capitalism, also innate, is that the rich get richer and the poor get poorer. To a certain extent this is a trend in any system but capitalism ensures that inequality is hard-wired in the fundamental mechanism. If you have excess income, you can invest to gather more, not by lending but owning a share, which is worth more as the company grows. The effect snowballs and the result is extraordinary. **2018 figures show that 26 people owned the same as the 3.8 billion people who make up the poorest half of humanity.** (Figures from Oxfam).

The problem with this systematic gathering of wealth is twofold. In the first place, power and influence grow with disposable income, to the point where individuals could buy whole countries and potentially become dictators. Where then is democracy?

In the second place, as people at the bottom become poorer, they lose buying power, so the markets that make the rich wealthy tend to shrink. This is a practical reason to control capitalism, not one dictated by ideology or emotion.

Looking now at the systems that we call socialist, the basis is one of fairness rather than greed. It is impossible to argue that fairness is intrinsically wrong but history tends to indicate that socialist systems work reasonably well until an inspirational leader gets too old to govern. There is then a power struggle and generally the new leader is not as idealistic as the old one. In some cases the incomer may be controlled by those with selfish intentions. Sometimes the new leader is a psychopath, like Stalin in the Soviet Union.

The pragmatic solution is to insist that the economy should be mixed, as most developed countries have decided. Even the most devoutly capitalist regimes have a need to gather taxes, to spend money on the army. Like it or not, this is a weak form of socialism. As individuals we are taxed to pay for something of benefit to the whole community.

I see no reason why the arguments for and against capitalism should not be discussed in schools at the secondary level. Surely a better-informed electorate is likely to make better decisions?

Anthropology: the hunter-gatherer

The time that has passed since 'civilisation' began is very short in evolutionary terms, maybe 5000 years or a little longer, compared to the hundreds of thousands of years taken to develop modern man. This time period can be taken to be even greater if we include the millions of years that it took to form the first primates.

During the process leading to *Homo sapiens*, social groups were small, typically 20-50 individuals, about the size of the hunter-gatherer units that still exist around the world, and of chimpanzees. In groups of this size, everybody knows everybody. They know their strengths and weaknesses, their attitudes and their foibles; there are no strangers except when they meet another group.

Knowing a relatively small number of people really well is good for survival; members of the group trust each other and rely on each other. Personal relationships are inbuilt in the small group and do not require social workers. This is the most natural way for human beings to live, hard wired into our psyche.

In a city, we mix with thousands of strangers every day, unless we hide indoors. Frequently, we respond by keeping ourselves to ourselves, refusing to form relationships with anybody except partners and family. This narrow selection of social contacts does not satisfy the inner requirement for a group with a common purpose. How else can you explain the willingness of a well-paid office worker to join the local rugby club and turn up on a cold, wet Sunday morning to play for the fifth team, and to dive into the base of a ruck to get the ball, risking injury? To do so is madness, unless the team fills the role of the missing social group. The urge to follow the genes must be very strong.

In the wild, social groups are necessary to find food and to protect the group against predators, or occasionally against other clans. Typically, we form strong emotional attachments within the group; members of a fighting platoon of soldiers may sacrifice their own lives for their comrades. This is a natural response, following millions of years of natural selection; in the wild, such groups tend to survive.

How does this relate to survival in the modern world? In the first place we are happiest, as a species, when we have a group of close friends with common goals, people that share experiences and in some cases food. Without social contact we tend to become lonely and depressed, resorting to pharmaceuticals or alcohol. We also set great store by possessions, known sometimes as 'retail therapy'.

At one time, when families of eight or more were the norm, the family group provided some of the social interactions that we crave. As a generalisation, the family group has not been replaced and we social animals become isolated and confused. Many efforts are made to overcome the effects of isolation, with local success, but the problem is huge. Even school friends tend to scatter and lose touch.

It is possible that Facebook, Snapchat and so on can partly fill the void; presumably their popularity is a result of the desperate need for people not to be alone, but there are problems with electronic communication. Telling your best friend about your private affairs is one thing but putting intimate details on line is another.

If we are to address the situation more generally, we could start by acknowledging that we are animals of a particular kind, selected over millions of years to behave in certain ways. Towns and cities are the biggest problem, when living units are not sited alongside other facilities that promote socialisation. Easterhouse, one of the new developments built to house people from the old Glasgow tenements that had no inside toilets, is a classic example. With the best intentions but no recognition of the human needs, the result was in some ways worse than the run-down neighbourhoods that were demolished.

I am not suggesting that top-down social engineering is required, it is more a requirement for making the living space more human, which means more flexible, allowing people to follow their ancient instincts.

The greenhouse effect

I come to this subject, not from the viewpoint of a meteorologist making global measurements of sea temperature and the disappearance of the polar ice caps, but as a laboratory worker.

As a student I had to record data about the compounds I made, using spectroscopy: specifically ultra-violet and infra-red. We talk about 'visible light' and 'ultraviolet light' and we could just as well refer to 'infrared light', although this is much less common. They are all forms of electromagnetic radiation and the sun produces a full range.

In the lab, I quickly learned that I could not use an ordinary glass cell to record either UV or IR data, because ordinary glass blocks almost everything except visible light. For UV I had to use a special kind of silica glass and for IR I could not use glass at all. Instead, I had to use rock salt plates, for a liquid, and a mix of salt and my compound, compressed into a disc, for a solid.

In a greenhouse we tend to use cheap glass, which lets in visible light and not much else. Why, then, does the greenhouse warm up? The effect is clearly noticeable even on cloudy days.

The answer is that visible light hits everything inside the greenhouse: some is reflected, which is useful as we can see what is there, but much is absorbed. When visible light is absorbed it gets turned into heat and the warm object radiates infra-red light back out, but the IR cannot escape; instead it is absorbed by whatever is in the greenhouse and warms up. The contents get warmer and the heat is trapped.

Something similar happens when light hits the earth. Visible and UV light pass through the atmosphere, are absorbed and re-emitted as IR. The IR tends to be absorbed by carbon dioxide and methane in the atmosphere and by water vapour. The biggest component of our atmosphere is nitrogen but this is much less capable of absorbing IR. If we increase the atmospheric content of any gas that absorbs IR, the earth gets warmer.

What has this to do with education? Unless we teach the basic science to school children and adults, supported by simple practical demonstrations, we risk the 'climate sceptics' sabotaging any rational attempt to avoid the consequences of our own actions. Politicians, around the world, are susceptible to bribery by those who stand to lose from a move to clean energy. The bribery may not be personal, it could simply be a call to economic interest or international competition, but the effect is the same: muddle and delay.

It would not be difficult to devise a demonstration of the greenhouse effect that children could organise themselves; remember the Chinese 'I do and I understand'. For many teachers a personal acquaintance with the effect would be beneficial but I would suggest that the children should be made responsible, rather than follow a protocol that someone else has laid on a plate. All it needs is two glass boxes, two thermometers, a small supply of dry ice and preferably a cloudy day. I leave the details to you.

I can imagine the establishment saying 'The greenhouse effect is already covered in module X' but this misses the point. In the first place, the practical investigation may be missing, actually showing the large variation in temperature that can occur. More widely, global warming has impacts on all aspects of life on the planet, from biology to economics, and should be taught in this way.

Generalities

Exam technique

I have occasionally been asked to help students who were struggling with the usual factoid overload. They were invariably intelligent but not gifted with the best memory and could get desperate to prove that they were not thick.

The first step is to acknowledge the problem and then to change your revision technique. The words I used were 'Be as hard on yourself as the examiner will be'. In a system that relies on memory it is no good just reading something and understanding it, you have to be able to regurgitate the factoids in an exam answer.

The way to do this, in my experience, is to read a passage of text or diagrams, or whatever other format was used, then to close the book (or laptop, tablet or whatever) and write down what you can remember. Compare this with your source and see what you have left out. You will soon see what your examiner would see; an absence of detail. It is the detail that earns the high marks, not the understanding.

If we change the way that we teach and examine, this advice will not be necessary. Change will eventually come, I hope, but in the meantime you will have to be pragmatic.

The year in education

Most people are probably unaware that the academic year at Oxford and Cambridge is divided into three eight-week terms. This suited the young gentlemen of previous centuries, who were free to take a tour of Europe in the summer and to go grouse shooting in August. They certainly did not spend the summer learning anything practical.

Since exams take place during term time, the teaching year is well short of 24 weeks. This is particularly interesting in a culture that insists on cramming facts into schoolchildren for more than 40 weeks in a year. It is also significant that somebody choosing PPE (Politics, Philosophy and Economics) can go straight into a political career. If we assume that the three subjects get an equivalent proportion of time, each will have been studied for a total of rather less than 24 weeks in the whole of the three years normally taken for an undergraduate degree. On this basis, if they choose, they can end up taking decisions for the whole country.

There is an inconsistency here: either the Oxbridge graduate is inadequately prepared for modern life, which may well be true, or we confine our children to classrooms for far too long, which is certainly true. We can see very clearly that much of what goes on in schools is really child-minding.

The cult of celebrity

For reasons that escape me, our world culture requires that certain people should be singled out for special praise. The Nobel prizes are an extreme example but it happens constantly in all the media. The problem is that those awarding the accolades are usually unaware of who did what. An outstanding example is the award of the Nobel prize for the discovery of quasars, a kind of star that sends out regular pulses of radiation, to the PhD supervisor and not the student who did the work and stuck at it in the face of discouragement. In a cultural sense the tendency to give all the credit to one person follows our habit of saying, for example, that Henry VIII built Hampton Court Palace or Tutankhamun built the valley of the kings.

Many years before quasars were discovered, a graduate in medicine who noticed a clear ring around a mould on a plate of jelly, in which bacteria were growing, received not only the Nobel prize but a knighthood. Alexander Fleming is widely credited with discovering penicillin, although he had neither the education nor the experience to do so. He himself referred to the 'Fleming Myth'.

In more recent times, the BBC has interviewed experts on climate change. To make the interview more lively, they would also bring in Nigel Lawson, who is not a scientist, let alone a weather expert, but he argued that climate change was not real. He was at one time chancellor of the exchequer, under Margaret Thatcher.

Even more recently, when Stephen Hawking became famous as a mathematician, working in astrophysics, he began to be asked for his views about anything that affected mankind. There is no doubt that he was a brilliant and imaginative mathematician but some of his ideas were potty. For example, he was pessimistic about the future for the earth but his conclusion was not that we must learn to live differently but that we should invent a matter/antimatter engine, to allow us to reach other solar systems.

Take a few minutes to analyse this suggestion. First, nobody has a clue how to make such an engine; there is no existing technology. Second, the distances to other solar systems are mind-boggling. Suppose that we wish to visit the nearest star system, about four light years away. Imagine that we have invented a space ship that can travel at ten million miles per hour. At present we can get nowhere near that but just suppose....

Light travels at 186,282 miles per second or 670,616,629 mph. If we travel at 10 million mph it will take 67 years to cover the distance taken by light in one year. Four light years will take 268 years!

If we got there, we would not know if any of the circling planets could support life. On the way, at 10 million mph a collision with even a tiny object would be terminal. *Perhaps it would be better to keep our planet habitable as long as possible.* The only people stopping us are politicians, who seem incapable of grasping the reality of global warming.

The point of all this is that experts are knowledgeable in very restricted areas. If we wish to know about subjects that may impact on all of us we should learn directly from specialists about their own subject, perhaps through an intermediary who can translate the jargon into normal English, not an easy task. Even then, remember that experts often disagree.

The relevance to my general theme is simple. Much education is for oneself, by oneself, which underlines the importance of scepticism. Do not believe in opinions from single sources and treat all branches of the media with suspicion, particularly the internet. There is a tendency for undergraduates to believe, without question, anything that is printed in book form. It might be beneficial if they all read 'Lies my teacher told me'.

Overseas aid

I am sticking to the book title here, not getting involved with the generality of richer countries giving money to less fortunate ones.

To begin, some simple calculations. The average number of children per couple in Africa is five. This figure has not changed for many years and has led to unprecedented levels of population growth. As an example, the population of Kenya was 8 million in 1948, the first time there was a census. In 1987, the first time I visited Kenya, the population was 25 million and it was growing by one million a year.

If you wonder what impact this has had on the people of Kenya, I suggest that you read Jomo Kenyatta's autobiography, which describes village governance among the Kikuyu. Although population growth was not a pressing problem in Kenyatta's time, his book permits an understanding of the current situation. For a community that relies on subsistence farming the huge growth in population means that second and later sons have to leave the village and seek their fortune elsewhere. For many, this means living in one of the enormous slums that now disfigure Nairobi. They have a hand-to-mouth existence.

To a calculation. Suppose that we have a community of just 64 couples in a village in Kenya. Recent figures show that each couple, on average, has five children so there are now 448 people trying to make a living from the same piece of land. Assuming that there are equal numbers of boys and girls and that they marry within the community, in the next generation there will be 160 young couples who each have five children. The new generation has 800 members. If life expectancy is not great and we assume that all the grandparents die relatively young, the community now numbers 1120. The population will have grown from 128 to 1120 in two generations.

Quite obviously, this population figure cannot be supported and does not happen. We can guess that there is substantial loss of life through disease and accident, with relatively poor levels of health care in a poor country. Migration to the city will also slow population growth, because an unemployed man cannot offer to support a wife and may never get married.

We still see enormous numbers of very poor people trying to eke out an existence, with little dignity and no prospects. Crime levels are high.

Under these circumstances I cannot understand African politicians, one or two of whom claim that population control is 'dangerous'. Some Africans believe that foreigners are 'trying to keep the Africans down'. History and present reality suggest the opposite.

Population growth in Europe, for at least 200 years up to World War II, was enormous, similar to that in Africa today. Conditions in the cities were tough. For the poor, who were the great majority, it was a constant struggle to survive and life expectancy was very low.

At least three factors contributed to a change of fortune for the very poor. First, contraception became a practical possibility with the invention of condoms and other devices. Second, women were more likely to be educated and third, the shortage of manpower following heavy losses in World War I meant that women changed their role in society, doing work that was previously reserved for men. This included driving trucks and flying aeroplanes.

With greater confidence, women started to have a say in the conduct of family affairs, which included freedom from getting pregnant every two or three years. With reasonably priced contraception normal conjugal relations could be maintained, which eased frustration levels for both sexes.

In the developing world, the woman's role has not changed; she is still expected to look after the children as number one priority, grow and prepare food, fetch water and look after the old people. Generally they are dominated by the men, who themselves are poorly educated.

In Africa, a man's status is affected by the number of children he fathers. This may have been a part of the community's survival strategy in past times but in the 21st Century it is out of date. Many more people survive to have children of their own and, through the adoption of various elements of the way of life of richer countries, more children survive. For example, smallpox has been eradicated and polio is much less common.

If the developed world wishes to help the poor in other places, the first and most effective step is to improve education generally and specifically for women, who need to know how women live in developed countries. Typically, they need to be able to read and write and do 'sums'. Just like people in the UK.

Without education, women in Africa will be unable to play a full part in their future and that of their children. They will be condemned to a life of drudgery, with the added misery of watching their children die from malnutrition.

There are a number of charities dedicated to the development of women's rights in Africa and elsewhere. Unfortunately, the biggest charities in the UK, such as 'Save the Children' and Oxfam, have traditionally seen their role as providing food and water and no more. The result is that communities remain ignorant and grow even faster. It would help to avoid or lessen future disasters if the big charities would take some responsibility for the quality of life of those they have 'saved'. The alternative is to have to go back in a few year's time and feed even more starving people. Most educated women choose to have smaller families.

The argument presented thus far is entirely philanthropic but there is a benefit in return for the developed world. At present there are millions of people around the world who are not prospering as they would wish. They see life in Europe and the USA as having many advantages. Not least is health care but they also see a possibility of getting work in a community that is more regulated and safer, as well as generally more prosperous.

A second benefit of population control, not often recognised, lies in the potential to reduce the number of unemployed and unmarried young men. Socially and sexually frustrated, they are ripe for exploitation. I don't suppose that anybody knows why young men from England would choose to join a band of murderous thugs creating mayhem in the Middle East, but I will guess. The prospect of fighting for a cause with a band of religious brothers is the excuse but in their imaginations they may have thought that they would be able to dominate: to have sex with any woman they chose, to learn how to kill at will and be untouchable. On top of that, they would be paid by wealthy fanatics. In other words, with no real purpose in life, joining IS would be an adventure.

Some citizens of the developed world argue that migration has always happened and they are right. What they do not see is that the pressure to migrate is greater now than it has ever been. Trying to accommodate all those who wish to migrate from Africa, let alone Asia and the Middle East, is like trying to drain one of the North London reservoirs into a garden pond.

Who can wonder that they wish to migrate? As long as they see that life is better in the developed world, young men in particular will try to move. The pressure on the developed world as conditions worsen in poorer countries will increase to the point where there will be a backlash, a fertile environment for the extreme right to step in. There are already signs that this may happen in several European countries, as well as the USA.

Every time I visit the South of England I wonder at the poor quality of life that residents have there. As well as long commutes to work, expensive housing and increasing violence, there is simple population pressure. Car parks are often full, long traffic delays are normal and even national parks like the New Forest in Hampshire are grossly overcrowded, not at all the quiet country environment they once were.

I spent all of my formative years in what is now called Waltham Forest, between north-east London and Essex. I lived in Chingford and went to school in Walthamstow. When describing where I came from, to people from the rest of Britain who had never heard of Chingford, I would always say that it was one of the most boring places on the planet. Not unpleasant but with little for a teenager to do. I regularly walked home from Walthamstow, a distance of about three miles, having spent the evening with friends. There was never any trouble; the thought never occurred to me. Now apparently there are eleven drug gangs operating in the borough, one of them run by people of Somali origin. The ethnicity of the gangs has been documented in an academic study ('From postcodes to profit. How gangs have changed in

Waltham Forest', by Andrew Whittaker et al., through Google).

With net migration into the UK still running at well over 200,000 every year, the situation can only get worse. It is no wonder that there is a shortage of housing.

The developing world needs to be made aware of the catastrophe that awaits the entire planet, if habits do not change. Climate change is caused by people and 'more people' means more climate change. We can carry on as before, with an absolute guarantee that hundreds of millions of people will die from starvation as productive land dries up and low-lying areas are flooded, or we can try to educate for survival.

Having children

It was recognised many years ago that sex education is important for children in the UK, to abandon the kind of Victorian prudishness that led to young women getting pregnant through ignorance. For children in their teens to attempt to raise children of their own is not feasible; they do not have the resources.

There is a possibility that children who are encouraged to discuss sexual intercourse will also be encouraged to try it for themselves, so the way that the subject is approached needs to be carefully judged. A complicating factor in the 21st Century is the ready availability of pornography, which may have the effect of making sex seem no more than routine, no more emotional than eating a meal. In normal human relationships there are some powerful subconscious drivers that teenagers may not understand. This requires a very sensitive approach from teachers that I am not competent to discuss.

In much of the less developed world there is widespread ignorance about sexuality. In Africa, for example, there is a common belief among men that they must have regular sex or they will lose the ability. This is coupled to a cultural image of the real man as someone who fathers lots of children.

Everywhere that women are educated, the birth rate drops. As Sir David Attenborough once said to an invited audience, educated women can see that feeding four children is a lot easier than feeding ten. In Kerala, a state in southern India where there is 97% adult literacy, the birth rate is at the same level as in Europe. Some years after Robert Mugabe became president of Zimbabwe the level of adult literacy was the highest in Africa. The birth rate was the lowest in Africa. The figures speak for themselves and it is unfortunate that economic mismanagement in Zimbabwe has since seen a rise in the birth rate, although it is still substantially lower than in surrounding countries.

Charities are constantly called upon to feed people in poorer countries. When they do so, they interrupt the natural cycle of feast and famine that has occurred over the centuries. In 1984, President Mengistu of Ethiopia remarked that famine was a natural means of population control, a heartless remark considering that thousands of his own people were starving to death.

Common sense tells us that the charities are adding to future problems if they do not help to educate the people that they are feeding. In the 21st Century nobody would echo Thomas Malthus's remedy for over population, that the children of the poor should be allowed to starve. In his day, there was no reliable means of birth control.

Leisure

It occurred to me on re-reading the earlier chapters that I may have given an impression that I look on all learning as either financially beneficial or a waste of time. At the same time, I realised that over many years Louis Armstrong had been more important to me than Albert Einstein. At times, listening to music has had survival value.

When life is tough and the main priority is putting food on the table it may be unwise to spend much time playing, but for most people, once they can eat and find shelter, thoughts turn to other things and not just sex. Education can make leisure time more rewarding if it is approached in the right way, by introducing people to new things. As a rule we are not attracted to activities that are unfamiliar.

There has been a tendency to impose a merit order on leisure activities, even music. Beethoven was regarded as 'superior' to the Beatles, for example, without a shred of evidence. The best music, and the most difficult to write, is often the simplest. Some complex music can become accessible, and therefore enjoyable, when it becomes familiar. Duke Ellington and Billy Strayhorn wrote some stuff that sounds very strange at first. I remember buying a vinyl LP of the Ellington band when I was a teenager and thinking that I had wasted my money. From time to time I played it again and started to enjoy the strange harmonies. I now think of those recordings as pure genius. You could call it accidental self-education.

It is unfortunate that so much snobbery is attached to so many kinds of artistic output. I am convinced that many members of the 'establishment', the kind of people who sometimes end up on 'Desert Island Discs', have no feeling for music at all. With some of them, conscious of their social status, I would guess that their choice of music is provided by somebody else, invariably 'classical'. Anything rhythmic is regarded with suspicion, at best a guilty pleasure to be enjoyed behind closed doors.

One of the problems with accessibility is that a proportion of the output of the leisure industry is pretentious rubbish. A favourite ploy, when you have run out of original ideas, is to make the music more complicated or technically more difficult. I would say that Charlie Parker was guilty of this, as was Paganini. Alternatively, when faced with earning a living and having to supply another piece, the composer has to produce another pot-boiler. Tin Pan Alley does this all the time, and so did Mozart. I don't blame either of them.

Education with the aim of enriching leisure time has to cover a wide range, not just repeated exposure to the teacher's favourites.

As with music, paintings vary from the easily accessible - 'The Haywain' for example - to some work by Picasso that convinces me that he had a sense of humour and was taking the mickey out of the 'experts'. While I would not wish a teacher to be too selective I think that expression of opinion should be encouraged. For example, the Museum of Modern

Art in New York has a few exhibits that, in my opinion, serve only to illustrate the gullibility of the art establishment.

I have never been able to understand the requirement to prove that a painting was attributable to a certain artist before attaching a price. The work is what it is; either you like it or you don't. If you can't say who painted it, who cares? Much of the nonsense attached to pricing works of art stems from the desire of very wealthy people to convert cash into something that will retain its value, regardless of inflation. Very often their purchases are stored in bank vaults, negating the whole purpose of visual art, which is obviously to be seen.

'Leisure' covers much more than art. Even football, in its highest form, appeals to the audience in a way that transcends mere physical activity. The same can be said of many other active expressions of human capability. A game of cricket can be far more than just running about, hitting and throwing a ball. Some of those who claim to be aesthetes, devoted to the performing arts, do not realise that there are whole parts of the human experience that they are missing.

External factors

Immigration

Human beings have always migrated. In prehistoric times we can imagine the circumstances that might have led to a compulsion to move; a change of climate could do it, if the rains failed. A growth in the numbers of aggressive neighbours would be another reason, when you might be faced with a choice between fighting or moving. Good living conditions might, paradoxically, lead to an exodus as the population rises and competition for resources increases. As long as there are differences in living standards between countries there will be pressure for movement but the rate at which movement occurs is important: if it is very slow nobody notices.

In the earliest human times people had to walk. The rate of movement was increased by sailing ships so that millions of people could be transported around the globe, when population growth in Europe made life uncomfortable. As always, migration is good for the migrant and with few exceptions bad for the indigenous people. Think of the North American 'Indians', the aborigines in Tasmania who were wiped out and the Bushmen of Southern Africa who could be legally shot, on the basis that they were not really human.

The UK should be well placed to limit movement if it wishes but there are powerful forces in favour of migration into the country. If you are an international company wishing to increase profits by opening a chain of hotels in Britain, the prospect of employing immigrants on low wages is very attractive. The advantage to the migrant is obvious but the pressure to migrate is often misrepresented as coming solely from wars or persecution, both powerful incentives. In many cases the attraction is simply to find work and escape is only available to young men with enough money to pay the traffickers.

As an aside, the Middle East has seen the co-existence of ethnic and religious groups for centuries, mutually supportive and tolerant. Only recently has this descended into tribal conflict, coinciding with a huge population increase and a desperate competition for work.

Even if immigration were banned, the UK borders are leaky, despite the large moat that surrounds these islands. Traffickers find ways of bringing young women for the sex trade by bribing lorry drivers, others find their way through the airports on forged documents, and there are plenty of people prepared to provide small boats to get across the channel, at a price. Add to these the people from Eastern Europe who have arrived in tens of thousands in recent years and the pressure on accommodation, schools and services such as the NHS has increased. At the time of writing, in some parts of England patients who are in pain have been told that they cannot get a doctor's appointment for three weeks.

In schools around London it is not unusual to have classes in which the number of languages spoken is in double figures. Although the mix may be stimulating, the challenge to maintain teaching standards has an extra complication.

On top of the communication problem, there are ethnic differences in the attitudes to school. Surveys show that poor white and black boys tend to be less inclined to take school seriously, while children from a variety of Asian countries do well.

There is little xenophobia among young children. Most often the kids get on very well with each other and tend to be colour blind, but somehow we need to find ways of getting the best from all of them. The alternative, in the inner cities, is for the early school leavers to be unable to find employment; some end up in drugs gangs, with the prospect of a violent life and an early death.

This scenario leads right back to the necessity for teaching methods to be tailored to the children: it does not work the other way round. The problem is the same as for kids from the same cultural background but with different aptitudes, with the further complication of social factors linked to ethnicity.

Drugs

Drug taking has increased enormously since the 'swinging sixties'. It was known as 'drug abuse' until the last few decades when, for reasons that are not clear, it started to be called 'drug use'. This change of name makes it slightly more acceptable to some sections of society, who started to experiment.

At the time of writing it has been estimated, from chemical analysis of sewage water, that there may be about 200,000 people in London who regularly 'use' cocaine. Even a member of the government has admitted to snorting cocaine at parties attended mainly by journalists. There is a health risk in so doing but the major problem is not the 'user' but the transfer of large amounts of cash to dealers, who fight for the local market.

The establishment attitude to cocaine abuse has been to ignore the 'user' and focus on the dealers, an approach that has not worked in controlling the market or its side-effects.

When relatively wealthy people pay for their cocaine they cause mayhem in local communities. Gang violence increases as local gang leaders compete for the market. Young men are stabbed to death, some are shot: they may be as young as fourteen. Involvement in gangs is often compulsory for innocent kids living on housing estates controlled by the drug gangs. The children may have to prove their allegiance to the gang master by gratuitous acts of violence. All of this arises from stupid better-off members of society looking for a brief thrill on a Saturday night.

If these supposedly respectable members of society are not aware of, or don't care what effect their drug habits have on fellow human beings, it is time they were educated. If they fail to respond it is time for a change of government policy. Rather than futile pursuit of the gang leaders, who are in and out of prison and don't care, the 'users' should be pursued, brought to court and exposed to public examination.

These well-off 'users' are responsible for many deaths and widespread misery.

Health and Safety

In many places of work there are dangers, sometimes from machinery and sometimes from chemicals. Deep sea fishing is very dangerous when the weather is rough, farming has hazards from livestock and machinery.

We do not ban fishing or farming, because we need the food. Building sites are dangerous but we need housing for people and industries. It would be ridiculous to ban all potentially dangerous activities but this is exactly what we do in education. Instead of teaching students to control danger by good practice, we tend to refuse permission.

Not only does this disrupt research, it fails to teach an essential aspect of safe behaviour, which is to manage risk so that it ceases to be a threat.

In Manchester I started a line of research that involved volatile sulphur compounds, which are incredibly smelly. They are so smelly that human beings can detect them at one part in fifty billion, which is why a tiny quantity is added to North Sea gas so that leaks can be detected.

One of my students used this kind of chemistry to great effect but the first time, in the hazardous reactions laboratory, he washed a tiny quantity down the sink. About an hour later the university library was evacuated with everybody convinced there was a gas leak. The student changed his technique and we avoided the problem thereafter.

Much later, with really miniscule quantities of a similar compound, in another university, I was instructed to stop what I was doing altogether. The message came from the head of Health and Safety and I stopped immediately, but it did occur to me that nobody asked if the work was important.

Epilogue

Having got this far, I realised that I had made no mention of happiness, even though there is a direct connection with survival. Since the context is 'education', I puzzled over whether it is possible to teach people to be happy.

Although many families have more disposable income than they have ever had, the proportion of the population who are taking anti-depressants keeps going up. Self-harm among teenagers is more common now than when I was young and so is suicide. This does not suggest that people are happier.

Curiously, people who are struggling to survive tend to concentrate on tackling the immediate problem, whether that is finding enough to eat or sheltering from the cold. It is as if they are built to withstand hard times, psychologically as well as physically, to fight whatever is pushing them towards oblivion. When those pressures are removed they have more time to think and worry, often about trivia.

Since the invention of broadcasting, it has been possible to spread news from one part of the world to all the others. For reasons that are not entirely clear, the news organisations have become obsessed with tragedy. If it is not a landslide in the Philippines it is the collapse of a dam wall in Brazil, forest fires in California or the destruction of rain forests all over the world.

In the UK, we may be told that the wheat harvest is going to be ruined by prolonged rainfall or that the yields of potatoes are way down because the weather has been too dry. In the years when the rain falls at just the right time and there is a bumper harvest, we hear nothing. Except that there is a drought in Africa and millions of people are facing starvation.

In recent years we have been encouraged to buy diesel cars, because they use less fuel and produce less carbon dioxide. Jaguar-Landrover spent a fortune developing a diesel engine that is even more efficient. Then we find that exhaust emissions from diesel engines cause lung disease in cities and J-L have to lay off hundreds of workers from their production lines.

Is there any wonder that we are miserable? It is not surprising that people are drinking too much and dying from liver damage at an early age, or gambling on the internet, or turning to drugs. When they turn to drugs they damage their own health and give money to violent gangs who fight each other for market share, so that previously peaceful neighbourhoods turn into no-go areas, in which guns and knives are carried for self-protection.

And always the big black cloud of climate change threatens to make life impossible for millions.

Whoopee!

If education can help at all, it must be to give children hope. Actually, not just children. Ian Dury's song 'Reasons to be cheerful Part 3' may be a place to start. There are lots of things to be glad about, if you can be bothered to think. As well as looking on the bright side, or even looking to see if there is a bright side, there are a few basic aspects of life on earth that need attention. If we could get these sorted out we could be on the road to a better life for all:

population growth

climate change

wealth distribution

It will require a change from opportunism to wisdom, which is asking a lot of our politicians. At some point, we shall be in such a bad state that even the most stupid will no longer be able to argue that greed will solve all our problems. To bring about a change will require some extraordinary human beings, but as Ian Dury said 'There ain't arf bin some clever bastards'.

About the author

Roger Waigh was born near Loughborough in 1944, after his mother was evacuated from London where V2 rockets were landing.

After a few years in Leytonstone the family moved to Chingford, where he attended Chase Lane primary school. He passed the 11+ and progressed to the Sir George Monoux grammar school in Walthamstow. He asked to leave school at 16 but was persuaded by his father to stay on. He did not thrive in the sixth form but eventually managed to pass chemistry, botany, physics and zoology at 'A' level, the last two after resits.

He was fortunate to gain a place at the Bristol College of Science and Technology to study pharmacy, an external London degree, graduating in 1966. He then went straight to a PhD in the same college, which after one year became Bath University, studying organic chemistry. This was the first time he felt as if he was doing the right thing.

After graduating in 1969 he moved to a post-doctoral position at the University of Strathclyde in Glasgow and in 1970 transferred to a permanent lectureship. In 1976 he moved to a lectureship in the University of Manchester, teaching pharmacy students, and was promoted to senior lecturer. While in Manchester he was a pioneer of computer-assisted learning, with some financial assistance from the Pharmaceutical Society.

In 1991 he was invited back to Strathclyde University as Professor of Medicinal Chemistry. He is author or co-author of well over 100 scientific papers and in 2002 was awarded the degree of DSc by the University of Bath.

He was frequently asked to act as external examiner for undergraduate and post graduate taught courses, home and overseas, as well as for PhD's. He has taught as a visitor in University College London as well as in Malaysia, the Philippines and Nepal.

www.ingramcontent.com/pod-product-compliance
Lightning Source LLC
Chambersburg PA
CBHW060518100426
42743CB00009B/1369